Professional Ethernet: STP, RSTP, MSTP and TRILL

James Relington

DEDICATION

To those who seek knowledge, inspiration, and new perspectives—
may this book be a companion on your journey, a spark for curiosity,
and a reminder that every page turned is a step toward discovery.

AKNOWLEDGEMENTS

I would like to express my deepest gratitude to everyone who contributed to the creation of this book. To my colleagues and mentors, your insights and expertise have been invaluable. A special thank you to my family and friends for their unwavering support and encouragement throughout this journey.

Understanding Ethernet Switching Fundamentals

Ethernet switching lies at the very heart of modern computer networking, forming the foundational layer for both local area networks (LANs) and larger-scale enterprise environments. Before diving into advanced topics like spanning tree protocols or data center fabrics, it is crucial to understand how Ethernet switching operates at a fundamental level. The basic premise of Ethernet switching is to connect devices within the same broadcast domain and forward traffic based on MAC (Media Access Control) addresses. This function appears simple on the surface, but under the hood, it involves complex logic, tables, and real-time decisions that ensure efficiency, speed, and reliability in data transmission.

At its core, an Ethernet switch operates at Layer 2 of the OSI model. It uses MAC addresses to make forwarding decisions for frames arriving on its ports. When a device sends an Ethernet frame, it includes the destination MAC address, and the switch examines this information to determine where the frame should go. Initially, when a switch is powered on or reset, its MAC address table—also known as a forwarding table or CAM table—is empty. As frames are received, the switch inspects the source MAC address and the port on which the frame arrived, then dynamically learns which MAC addresses are reachable through which ports. Over time, the switch builds a map of the network, enabling it to intelligently forward unicast traffic only to the destination port rather than flooding it to all connected devices.

This dynamic learning process significantly reduces unnecessary traffic, which would otherwise flood the network, especially in larger environments. However, during the learning process, or in cases where a MAC address is unknown or has aged out, the switch will resort to flooding the frame to all ports within the same VLAN except the source port. This behavior ensures that the frame reaches its destination, even in the absence of a known path. While flooding is necessary in certain scenarios, it is generally kept to a minimum in well-functioning networks due to the switch's ability to rapidly learn and maintain an up-to-date forwarding table.

One of the essential concepts in Ethernet switching is the notion of collision domains and how switches isolate them. In early Ethernet networks built with hubs, all devices shared the same collision domain, meaning only one device could successfully transmit at a time. Collisions were frequent, and throughput suffered as a result. Ethernet switches resolved this by providing a dedicated collision domain for each switch port. This allowed for full-duplex communication, enabling devices to send and receive data simultaneously without interference. The move from hubs to switches marked a turning point in LAN performance and efficiency, making switched Ethernet the dominant standard in modern networks.

Another critical aspect of Ethernet switching is how broadcast and multicast traffic is handled. While unicast traffic is directed to a specific port, broadcast frames are sent to all ports within the same VLAN. Broadcasts are essential for certain network protocols, such as ARP (Address Resolution Protocol), but excessive broadcast traffic can degrade network performance. Multicast traffic behaves similarly, though it is typically more controlled through techniques like IGMP snooping, allowing switches to selectively forward multicast streams only to interested receivers. Understanding the implications of broadcast and multicast behavior is key to designing scalable and efficient networks.

Ethernet switches also support virtual LANs (VLANs), which allow network administrators to segment traffic logically rather than physically. VLANs are assigned to switch ports and act as separate broadcast domains. This segmentation provides benefits in terms of security, traffic management, and organizational structure. For example, different departments within a company can be assigned to different VLANs, isolating their traffic and reducing the scope of broadcasts. VLAN tags are inserted into Ethernet frames using IEEE 802.1Q tagging, which appends additional headers to identify the VLAN ID. Switches that support VLANs must be able to read, interpret, and forward traffic based on these tags, which adds a layer of complexity to switching behavior.

Switching fundamentals also encompass the concept of trunk ports and access ports. Access ports are typically assigned to a single VLAN and connect end-user devices, while trunk ports carry traffic for multiple VLANs across inter-switch links. Trunking is essential for extending VLANs across a network and maintaining consistent segmentation. To prevent issues like loops, which can arise when multiple switches are interconnected without proper control, additional protocols such as STP, RSTP, or MSTP are employed. These protocols ensure that a loop-free topology is maintained, even in redundant network designs.

Ethernet switching also brings up the topic of latency and forwarding methods. Switches can use different techniques to forward frames, including store-and-forward, cut-through, and fragment-free switching. Store-and-forward reads the entire frame and checks for errors before forwarding, which introduces a slight delay but ensures reliability. Cut-through begins forwarding as soon as the destination MAC address is read, reducing latency but at the risk of propagating corrupted frames. Fragment-free is a compromise, forwarding frames after the first 64 bytes, the minimum Ethernet frame size, to avoid forwarding runt frames. The choice of forwarding method can impact performance and is often determined by the specific requirements of the network.

In modern networks, Ethernet switches also incorporate Quality of Service (QoS) features to prioritize critical traffic, such as voice and video, over less time-sensitive data. QoS mechanisms may include traffic classification, queuing, and congestion management, all designed to ensure that high-priority packets are delivered in a timely manner. This becomes increasingly important in converged networks, where data, voice, and video coexist on the same infrastructure.

Ethernet switching is also evolving with the advent of software-defined networking (SDN), where control and data planes are decoupled. In an SDN-enabled switch, forwarding decisions can be made based on centralized policies, offering greater flexibility and programmability. While traditional Ethernet switches operate with built-in logic and decentralized control, SDN represents a shift toward intelligent, policy-driven networks that can adapt dynamically to changing requirements.

Grasping Ethernet switching fundamentals is a prerequisite for understanding more advanced technologies and protocols that build upon it. Whether dealing with loop prevention, virtualization, or data center fabrics, everything begins with the core principles of how switches learn, forward, and manage traffic. These foundational concepts shape the behavior of larger, more complex systems and are essential knowledge for any network professional.

The Evolution of Bridging Technologies

The development of bridging technologies has played a transformative role in the architecture and scalability of Ethernet networks. From the earliest days of shared Ethernet media to the sophisticated fabric designs of modern data centers, the evolution of bridging has been driven by the need for greater efficiency, scalability, fault tolerance, and control over Layer 2 domains. Initially, Ethernet networks were built using hubs, which were simple devices that broadcast every frame to all ports, creating a single collision domain. These early networks were inherently inefficient and suffered from frequent collisions, limited scalability, and security concerns due to the indiscriminate nature of frame delivery.

The introduction of network bridges marked the first major shift in Ethernet architecture. A bridge could connect multiple network segments and make forwarding decisions based on MAC addresses, effectively filtering traffic and reducing unnecessary transmissions. By learning which MAC addresses were reachable on which ports, bridges were able to forward frames only where needed, significantly improving performance. Each segment connected to a bridge formed a separate collision domain, allowing for more efficient communication. Bridges represented a step toward more intelligent and scalable Ethernet networks, laying the groundwork for more advanced Layer 2 switching technologies.

As networks continued to grow in complexity and size, the limitations of traditional bridges became apparent. Managing large broadcast domains and preventing loops required more robust solutions. This led to the standardization of the Spanning Tree Protocol (STP) by IEEE as 802.1D. STP allowed bridges to create loop-free topologies by disabling redundant paths, ensuring that there was always a single active path between any two nodes in the network. The protocol selected a root bridge and calculated the shortest path to the root from all other devices, blocking paths that could form loops. While STP greatly enhanced network stability, it came at the cost of slow convergence times and underutilized redundant links.

To address the shortcomings of STP, the networking industry introduced Ethernet switches, which functioned similarly to bridges but with far greater port density, performance, and intelligence. Switches brought the same basic principles of MAC address learning and forwarding but at scale and with more granular control. They also introduced features such as VLAN support, port-based filtering, and more sophisticated management capabilities. However, switches still relied on STP to prevent loops, which continued to be a bottleneck in environments that demanded fast convergence and high availability.

Recognizing the need for faster recovery times and more efficient use of redundant links, the IEEE developed the Rapid Spanning Tree Protocol (RSTP), standardized as 802.1w. RSTP retained the loop prevention model of STP but introduced new port roles and states to accelerate convergence. It also implemented mechanisms for quickly transitioning ports to forwarding states, allowing networks to recover from topology changes in a matter of seconds instead of minutes. RSTP marked a significant improvement over legacy STP and became the preferred loop prevention protocol in many enterprise networks.

As networks evolved to support more VLANs and complex topologies, the need for a more scalable and flexible protocol became evident. This led to the development of the Multiple Spanning Tree Protocol (MSTP), standardized as 802.1s. MSTP allowed multiple VLANs to be grouped into instances, each with its own spanning tree. By doing so, MSTP reduced the number of spanning trees required, which decreased the processing overhead on switches and allowed for more efficient use of network links. MSTP also enabled better traffic engineering by allowing different VLANs to use different paths through the network. This was particularly beneficial in large enterprise environments where performance and traffic distribution were critical concerns.

Despite these advancements, traditional spanning tree-based protocols continued to suffer from inherent limitations. Even with faster convergence and better VLAN handling, the fundamental model of disabling redundant paths to prevent loops limited the full potential of network bandwidth. In response, the IETF introduced Transparent Interconnection of Lots of Links (TRILL), a new Layer 2 routing protocol that combined the benefits of bridging and routing. TRILL replaced spanning tree protocols with a link-state routing protocol based on IS-IS, enabling all paths to be active and utilized for forwarding traffic. It also introduced features like equal-cost multipath (ECMP), faster convergence, and support for large-scale Ethernet fabrics.

TRILL represented a paradigm shift in bridging technologies by enabling Ethernet networks to behave more like Layer 3 routed networks while maintaining Layer 2 transparency. Instead of blocking links, TRILL calculated the best paths to all nodes in the network and used encapsulation to forward frames between TRILL switches, known as RBridges. This eliminated the need for spanning trees entirely and allowed for more scalable and efficient network designs. While TRILL adoption has been more common in data center environments and among specific vendors, its introduction demonstrated the growing convergence of Layer 2 and Layer 3 technologies.

In parallel to TRILL, other innovations like Shortest Path Bridging (SPB) emerged as alternative solutions to the same problem. SPB, standardized by IEEE as 802.1aq, also used IS-IS to calculate shortest paths and supported multipath forwarding and loop-free topologies. Like TRILL, SPB aimed to overcome the limitations of spanning tree protocols and offered a modern approach to Ethernet bridging. These advancements have given network architects a broader toolkit for designing scalable, resilient, and high-performance Layer 2 infrastructures.

Throughout the evolution of bridging technologies, one constant theme has been the balance between simplicity and capability. Early bridges were simple but limited. STP introduced essential stability but at the cost of performance. RSTP and MSTP improved upon that foundation, offering better convergence and traffic management. The leap to TRILL and SPB signaled a move toward truly dynamic and intelligent Layer 2 networks capable of meeting the demands of virtualization, cloud computing, and software-defined networking. The journey from basic MAC address filtering to complex path computation protocols reflects the growing sophistication of Ethernet networks and the critical role that bridging continues to play in the digital world.

MAC Address Learning and Forwarding

The ability of Ethernet switches to learn and forward based on MAC addresses is one of the most fundamental mechanisms that enables Layer 2 communication to function efficiently. Unlike simple hubs that broadcast all traffic to every connected device, switches operate intelligently, examining the MAC addresses within Ethernet frames and making real-time decisions about how to handle those frames. This process, known as MAC address learning and forwarding, is central to how switches reduce network congestion, enhance performance, and maintain organized and scalable local area networks.

When a switch receives an Ethernet frame on one of its ports, the first thing it does is inspect the frame's source MAC address. This address is recorded in the switch's MAC address table, also known as the content-addressable memory (CAM) table. The table stores the relationship between MAC addresses and switch ports, allowing the device to know which port a particular MAC address is reachable from.

This learning process is dynamic and continuous. As devices send traffic through the switch, the table is constantly updated to reflect the most recent path associated with each MAC address. If the same MAC address is later seen arriving on a different port, the table is updated to reflect the new association, ensuring accurate and current forwarding decisions.

The switch uses this learned information when deciding how to forward frames. If the destination MAC address in the incoming frame is already in the table, the switch forwards the frame only to the specific port associated with that address. This targeted delivery eliminates unnecessary traffic on other ports, unlike broadcast-based devices. This behavior is known as unicast forwarding and is a major contributor to the efficiency of switched Ethernet networks. If, however, the destination MAC address is not in the table, the switch does not know where to forward the frame. In this case, it performs a process called flooding, where the frame is sent out to all ports within the same VLAN except the one it arrived on. This ensures that the frame has the best chance of reaching its intended recipient, and once the destination device replies, its MAC address is also learned and added to the table.

This dynamic nature of MAC address learning allows networks to adapt rapidly to changes, such as devices moving to different ports or links being reconfigured. However, to maintain accuracy, entries in the MAC address table are subject to an aging timer. If a MAC address is not seen on the network for a specific period, it is removed from the table. This aging mechanism prevents the table from becoming stale or filled with inactive entries, which could lead to incorrect forwarding or unnecessary flooding.

In addition to unicast traffic, Ethernet also has to deal with broadcast and multicast frames. A broadcast frame has a destination MAC address of all ones, which signifies that the frame should be delivered to all devices within the broadcast domain. Switches treat broadcast frames similarly to unknown unicast frames, flooding them out all ports in the VLAN except the one it arrived on. Broadcasts are necessary for certain protocols, like ARP, but excessive broadcasting can negatively impact performance. Multicast frames are addressed to a specific range of MAC addresses reserved for multicast communication. In default configurations, switches flood multicast traffic in the same way as broadcasts unless advanced features like IGMP snooping are implemented, which help limit the distribution to only interested receivers.

MAC address learning and forwarding becomes more complex in environments with virtual LANs. VLANs logically segment the switch into multiple isolated broadcast domains, each with its own MAC address table. This means that the same MAC address could appear on multiple VLANs and be associated with different ports in each context. When a frame arrives, the switch must consider not only the MAC address but also the VLAN ID to determine the correct forwarding behavior. Trunk ports, which carry traffic for multiple VLANs between switches, include a VLAN tag in each frame to preserve this distinction across links. The switch processes these tags to maintain separation between VLANs and ensure that MAC address learning occurs within the correct context.

Switching performance is also influenced by the type of forwarding method used. Store-and-forward switching reads the entire frame before making a forwarding decision, allowing error checking and ensuring data integrity but introducing some latency. Cut-through switching, on the other hand, begins forwarding as soon as the destination MAC address is read, which reduces delay but carries the risk of propagating corrupted frames. Fragment-free switching is a compromise that starts forwarding after the first 64 bytes, the minimum Ethernet frame size, to avoid forwarding runt frames. The choice of forwarding method can affect not just performance but also the behavior of MAC address learning, particularly under conditions of congestion or error-prone links.

MAC address spoofing and security concerns also arise in networks where attackers may try to manipulate the MAC address learning process. For example, a malicious actor could flood the switch with frames from many fake MAC addresses, overwhelming the CAM table and causing it to enter a fail-open mode in which all frames are flooded. This condition, known as MAC flooding, allows the attacker to sniff traffic intended for other hosts. To counter such threats, modern switches implement security features like port security, which can limit the number of learned MAC addresses per port and trigger actions like shutting down the port or alerting administrators when suspicious activity is detected.

In environments where mobility and virtualization are prevalent, such as data centers and cloud networks, MAC address learning faces additional challenges. Virtual machines may move between physical hosts, causing their MAC addresses to appear on different switch ports dynamically. Switches must adapt quickly to these changes to maintain correct forwarding paths. Technologies like MAC mobility, dynamic ARP inspection, and EVPN have emerged to address these challenges and maintain the integrity of MAC learning in dynamic environments.

The process of MAC address learning and forwarding is more than a simple mechanism; it is the backbone of Layer 2 Ethernet switching. It enables intelligent traffic handling, minimizes unnecessary data flow, and creates an organized infrastructure that scales from small offices to global enterprise networks. As technologies evolve, the fundamental principles of MAC-based forwarding continue to serve as the reliable foundation upon which all modern Ethernet designs are built.

Broadcast Domains and Loop Prevention

Broadcast domains are a fundamental concept in Ethernet networking, shaping how traffic propagates through Layer 2 environments and influencing network design, scalability, and performance. A broadcast domain is a logical division within a network in which a broadcast frame sent by one device can be received by all other devices. This behavior is inherent to Ethernet's original design, where devices often rely on broadcasts to discover services, resolve addresses, and communicate with unknown peers. Protocols like ARP, DHCP, and certain routing advertisements all depend on the ability to send broadcast frames. While broadcasts are necessary for basic network operations, their unregulated spread can lead to inefficiencies and even serious network disruptions as the number of devices in a broadcast domain increases.

In a simple network with no segmentation, all devices connected to the same switch or group of interconnected switches belong to the same broadcast domain. When one device sends a broadcast frame, the switch forwards it out all other ports within the same VLAN, reaching every other device in the domain. This behavior is manageable in small environments, but in larger deployments, it can lead to broadcast storms, where the volume of broadcast traffic consumes bandwidth, overwhelms devices, and causes network degradation. To combat this, network administrators implement strategies to reduce the size of broadcast domains, typically using VLANs to logically separate groups of devices. Each VLAN acts as its own broadcast domain, containing the spread of broadcast traffic and improving overall efficiency and security.

However, segmenting the network into smaller broadcast domains introduces another challenge—maintaining interconnectivity between switches while ensuring there are no Layer 2 loops. Loops in a bridged Ethernet network can have catastrophic consequences. Since Ethernet frames do not have a time-to-live field like IP packets, they can circulate endlessly in a looped topology. This behavior can result in broadcast storms, where duplicated broadcast frames multiply rapidly and saturate the network. Additionally, MAC address tables on switches become unstable as the same MAC address is seen on multiple ports, leading to constant updates and erratic forwarding behavior. As a result, even a single loop can render a network unusable in seconds.

To prevent these issues, Ethernet networks use loop prevention mechanisms, the most prominent of which is the Spanning Tree Protocol (STP). STP was developed to detect and eliminate Layer 2 loops by placing some switch ports into a blocking state, effectively pruning the topology into a loop-free tree. STP operates by electing a root bridge and calculating the shortest path to the root from every other switch. Ports that are not part of the shortest path are blocked, preventing frames from circulating endlessly. This ensures that each broadcast domain remains functional and loop-free, even in complex mesh topologies with redundant links.

While STP effectively solves the problem of loops, it introduces trade-offs. One of the most significant limitations is that it disables redundant paths, leaving bandwidth unused and reducing fault tolerance. If a link goes down, STP can re-converge and unblock alternate paths, but this process can take several seconds in its original form. During this convergence period, parts of the network may become temporarily unreachable, which is unacceptable in environments that require high availability and real-time performance. These drawbacks led to the development of improved versions such as Rapid Spanning Tree Protocol (RSTP) and Multiple Spanning Tree Protocol (MSTP), which reduce convergence times and allow more flexible topologies, especially in VLAN-rich environments.

Another aspect of loop prevention is how switches handle flooded traffic, such as unknown unicast, broadcast, and multicast frames. Since these types of traffic are flooded to all ports within a VLAN, any Layer 2 loop can amplify them and cause a storm. Some switches implement storm control features, which monitor the level of broadcast or multicast traffic and suppress it if it exceeds a predefined threshold. This provides a second layer of defense, helping to mitigate the impact of broadcast storms even when loops occur. However, such mechanisms are reactive rather than preventive and should not be relied upon as a substitute for proper loop avoidance protocols.

In networks that span multiple switches and require both redundancy and high-speed convergence, loop prevention must be carefully balanced with performance and resilience. Technologies like TRILL and SPB have emerged to replace STP-based designs entirely by enabling multipath Layer 2 routing without loops. These protocols use link-state routing algorithms to calculate optimal paths and encapsulate Ethernet frames for safe transport across complex topologies. By eliminating the need to block redundant links, they maximize available bandwidth and provide faster recovery in the event of a failure. While not universally adopted, these technologies represent the future of loop prevention in large-scale Ethernet environments.

It is also important to understand the human element in loop prevention. Misconfigurations, such as connecting two switch ports with a cable without proper spanning tree configurations, are among the most common causes of loops in enterprise networks. Even a simple act, like plugging a misconfigured access point into two switches simultaneously, can introduce a loop if protections like BPDU Guard, Loop Guard, or PortFast are not correctly implemented. These features provide additional layers of loop prevention by enforcing proper behavior on access ports and monitoring for unexpected BPDU activity.

Designing a scalable and reliable Ethernet network requires a deep understanding of broadcast domains and the risks posed by loops. Reducing the size of broadcast domains through VLANs not only improves performance but also isolates problems, making troubleshooting easier. Loop prevention protocols ensure that redundant topologies can exist without compromising stability, but they must be carefully tuned to meet the needs of the environment. Whether using traditional STP or more advanced protocols, engineers must design networks that can tolerate faults, adapt quickly, and maintain operational integrity under a variety of conditions. The interaction between broadcast traffic and loop prevention remains one of the most critical considerations in modern Layer 2 networking, influencing everything from switch configuration to physical cabling and logical design.

The Spanning Tree Algorithm Explained

The Spanning Tree Algorithm is a cornerstone of Ethernet networking, developed to address one of the most critical problems in Layer 2 environments: loops. While redundant paths in a switched network are necessary for fault tolerance and resiliency, their presence also opens the door to broadcast storms, MAC table instability, and frame duplication. The Spanning Tree Algorithm, defined by the IEEE 802.1D standard as part of the original Spanning Tree Protocol (STP), provides a systematic method for detecting and logically disabling redundant links, ensuring a loop-free topology while preserving redundancy for failover purposes. Understanding how the Spanning Tree Algorithm operates is essential for any network professional who designs or manages Layer 2 infrastructures.

At the core of the algorithm is the principle of creating a tree-like structure that spans the entire network. In this structure, there is exactly one active path between any two switches. Redundant links exist physically but are placed into a blocking state by the algorithm to prevent loops. If an active link fails, one of the previously blocked links can be activated, restoring connectivity without manual intervention. The algorithm dynamically identifies which links to forward and which to block based on a combination of bridge identifiers, port costs, and path priorities.

The first step in the Spanning Tree Algorithm is the election of a root bridge, which serves as the central reference point for all path calculations. The election process is based on the bridge ID, which combines a configurable bridge priority value and the switch's MAC address. The switch with the lowest bridge ID becomes the root bridge. In practice, administrators often manually set the priority on a core switch to ensure it is elected as the root, thereby controlling the overall topology of the spanning tree.

Once the root bridge is elected, each switch in the network calculates the shortest path to the root. This calculation considers the path cost, which is based on the speed of the links traversed. Faster links have lower costs, and the switch chooses the path with the lowest cumulative cost to reach the root bridge. Each switch designates a single port as the root port, which is its best path to the root bridge. This port remains in a forwarding state, allowing traffic to flow toward the root.

For each network segment, the switch that provides the shortest path back to the root is designated as the segment's designated bridge, and the port it uses to reach that segment becomes the designated port. The designated port is also placed in the forwarding state, ensuring that traffic from that segment can reach the root efficiently. Any port that is neither a root port nor a designated port is placed in a blocking state. These ports do not forward frames, which prevents loops from forming while keeping the link available in case the active path fails.

The algorithm continuously monitors the network using Bridge Protocol Data Units (BPDUs), which are special frames sent by switches to share information about the network topology. BPDUs are used to detect topology changes, maintain the spanning tree, and ensure consistency across the network. When a switch receives a superior BPDU—one that advertises a lower-cost path to the root—it updates its configuration and may change its root port or designated ports accordingly. This real-time recalculation allows the spanning tree to adapt to changing conditions, such as link failures or the addition of new switches.

One of the challenges with the original Spanning Tree Algorithm is its slow convergence. When a topology change is detected, it can take up to 30 to 50 seconds for the network to fully stabilize, during which time some devices may be unreachable. This delay is primarily due to the various port states a switch must cycle through before a port transitions to forwarding. These states include blocking, listening, learning, and finally forwarding. Each state serves a purpose in the algorithm, preventing loops and allowing the switch to learn MAC addresses, but the overall process introduces latency that is undesirable in modern networks where high availability and low downtime are expected.

To mitigate these issues, enhanced versions of the Spanning Tree Algorithm were developed, such as Rapid Spanning Tree Protocol (RSTP) and Multiple Spanning Tree Protocol (MSTP), which retain the basic principles of the algorithm while optimizing convergence time and providing greater flexibility in complex topologies. However, even in its original form, the Spanning Tree Algorithm remains a robust and reliable method for managing redundant links and ensuring a stable Layer 2 environment.

The effectiveness of the algorithm depends heavily on proper configuration and understanding. Misconfigurations, such as incorrect bridge priorities or unbalanced path costs, can lead to suboptimal topology decisions that degrade performance. Additionally, without features like BPDU Guard or Root Guard, user actions such as connecting unauthorized switches can inadvertently disrupt the spanning tree and destabilize the network. Therefore, administrators must not only understand how the algorithm works but also implement best practices to maintain control over its operation.

In large enterprise environments, the design of the spanning tree becomes more strategic. Engineers must consider physical topology, bandwidth availability, and failure domains when selecting a root bridge and configuring link costs. Creating a deterministic and predictable spanning tree ensures that traffic takes the most efficient paths under normal conditions and recovers quickly during outages.

Moreover, integrating the spanning tree with other Layer 2 features such as VLANs, trunking, and link aggregation requires careful planning to avoid unintended interactions and performance bottlenecks.

The Spanning Tree Algorithm represents a foundational technology that has enabled Ethernet to scale from small workgroup networks to global enterprise infrastructures. Its ability to prevent loops, adapt to changes, and maintain a logical topology across physically redundant links has made it an indispensable tool in network design. Despite the emergence of newer technologies that offer faster convergence and greater efficiency, the algorithm's principles remain relevant and widely implemented. A thorough understanding of how it works, why it exists, and how it impacts traffic flow is essential for designing resilient, stable, and efficient Layer 2 networks.

Bridge Protocol Data Units and Their Role

Bridge Protocol Data Units, commonly referred to as BPDUs, are the vital communication mechanism that enables the operation of the Spanning Tree Protocol and its variants in Ethernet networks. These specialized frames are exchanged between switches to maintain a loop-free Layer 2 topology and to dynamically respond to changes within the network. Without BPDUs, the Spanning Tree Algorithm would be unable to detect loops, select a root bridge, or determine which ports should forward traffic and which should block. Understanding the structure, function, and significance of BPDUs is essential for grasping how Ethernet switches collaborate to avoid broadcast storms and ensure path redundancy without creating loops.

The primary purpose of BPDUs is to share essential topology information between switches in a Layer 2 network. Every switch participating in STP generates and transmits BPDUs at regular intervals. These messages include critical data such as the sender's bridge ID, the path cost to the root bridge, the root bridge ID, port identifiers, and various timing parameters like hello time, max age, and forward delay. By analyzing the contents of received BPDUs, switches make decisions about their own role in the spanning tree, including whether to accept another switch as the root, whether to update their own path cost to the root, and whether to change the role of any of their ports.

When a network first starts or a new switch joins the topology, each switch initially assumes that it is the root bridge and sends BPDUs advertising itself as such. As these BPDUs propagate through the network, switches compare the received information against their current understanding of the network topology. The selection of the root bridge is based on the lowest bridge ID, which is a combination of a configurable priority value and the switch's MAC address. The switch with the lowest bridge ID becomes the root, and its BPDUs are considered superior to all others. As a result, switches receiving a superior BPDU update their own understanding of the network and forward the better information downstream.

The iterative exchange of BPDUs continues until all switches have a consistent view of the root bridge and their own position within the network topology. Each switch identifies the port with the lowest cost path to the root and marks it as the root port. On each network segment, a designated port is selected to forward traffic toward the root. All other ports, which do not contribute to the shortest loop-free path, are placed into a blocking state to prevent loops. These forwarding and blocking decisions are based entirely on the data received in BPDUs, making these small but powerful frames the cornerstone of network stability at Layer 2.

BPDU communication is not limited to the initial topology setup. BPDUs are continually exchanged to monitor the health and consistency of the network. In classic STP, BPDUs are sent every two seconds by default from the root bridge and forwarded by all other switches. These periodic messages serve as a heartbeat for the network, confirming that the topology remains intact. If a switch stops receiving BPDUs on a port for a duration exceeding the max age timer, it considers that path to be invalid and initiates a re-evaluation of the spanning tree. This reactive behavior allows the protocol to adapt to network changes such as link failures, switch reboots, or topology reconfigurations, although the convergence process in traditional STP can take up to 50 seconds.

Rapid Spanning Tree Protocol introduces a key enhancement by allowing switches to generate and process BPDUs independently, rather than simply forwarding them from the root. This change allows faster detection of topology changes and more rapid convergence. RSTP uses a handshake mechanism involving proposal and agreement messages embedded in the BPDU structure to quickly transition ports to forwarding state without waiting for lengthy timers to expire. This improvement highlights the evolving role of BPDUs not only as static advertisements but as dynamic control messages that drive real-time network behavior.

In addition to their primary function in topology control, BPDUs can serve as early warning signals for misconfigurations or security issues. Features like BPDU Guard can be enabled on access ports to prevent accidental or malicious connection of switches. When a port configured with BPDU Guard receives a BPDU, the switch assumes that a bridge has been connected where only an end device should exist and shuts down the port to protect the network. Similarly, Root Guard prevents a switch from accepting a superior BPDU on certain ports, helping to maintain the intended root bridge and prevent topology manipulation. These protections rely entirely on the presence and interpretation of BPDUs to enforce policy and safeguard the spanning tree structure.

Another important aspect of BPDUs is their VLAN context. In networks using Multiple Spanning Tree Protocol, different spanning tree instances can be associated with different VLAN groups. MSTP BPDUs carry additional information to identify the instance and map VLANs accordingly. This allows more granular control over which links are active for different traffic types, providing better load balancing and resource utilization. In such environments, BPDUs not only convey the state of the network but also act as the vehicle for segmenting and organizing traffic flows.

While BPDUs are relatively small in size, the consequences of failing to manage or monitor them properly can be severe. If BPDUs are inadvertently filtered, misconfigured, or dropped by intermediary devices, the switch topology can become inconsistent or unstable. In worse cases, loops may form, causing broadcast storms that degrade or completely disrupt network operations. Ensuring that BPDUs are transmitted reliably and received where expected is a critical part of network health monitoring and troubleshooting.

Network engineers and administrators must also consider the role of BPDUs in environments that include virtualization and dynamic infrastructure. Virtual switches used in hypervisors may need to participate in spanning tree processes or, in some cases, be configured to ignore BPDUs altogether. Misalignment between physical and virtual switch configurations can lead to unexpected forwarding behavior or topology loops. Clear understanding of where and how BPDUs are generated, processed, and acted upon becomes even more vital in these complex environments.

BPDUs are far more than just frames passed between switches. They are the control language of spanning tree protocols, enabling dynamic network decisions, ensuring loop-free paths, and maintaining stability through change. Their simple format belies their critical importance, and their proper function is fundamental to the reliable operation of any switched Ethernet network. Understanding their role, behavior, and interaction with various spanning tree enhancements provides the foundation needed to master Layer 2 networking and to build robust, high-availability infrastructures.

STP Port States and Transitions

The Spanning Tree Protocol is designed to prevent Layer 2 loops in Ethernet networks by controlling which switch ports are allowed to forward traffic and which are blocked. A central component of this control is the set of port states defined by STP. These port states are not static; they represent phases in a carefully controlled transition process that determines whether a port is actively forwarding traffic or merely monitoring the network topology. Understanding the STP port states and how transitions between them occur is crucial to grasp how the protocol ensures a loop-free topology while maintaining redundancy and fault tolerance.

Each STP port state reflects the port's current role in managing network traffic and topology information. These states are Blocking,

Listening, Learning, Forwarding, and Disabled. The transitions between these states are not arbitrary; they are determined by the STP algorithm based on received Bridge Protocol Data Units, or BPDUs, and the state of the overall network topology. Each port begins in a default state and then progresses through a series of changes based on its role in the spanning tree, the election of the root bridge, and the cost of paths to that root bridge.

When a switch port is initialized or when STP detects a topology change, it enters the Blocking state. In this state, the port does not forward any frames, including user traffic or BPDUs. The purpose of the Blocking state is to prevent any possibility of a loop forming while the switch assesses its place in the network. The port, however, still listens for incoming BPDUs so that it can participate in the spanning tree calculation. Blocking is a passive state, but it is essential in the early stages of topology convergence to ensure that no loops are inadvertently introduced.

After a port has spent a defined amount of time in the Blocking state and STP determines that the port may play a forwarding role without causing a loop, it transitions to the Listening state. In this state, the port still does not forward user traffic, but it begins to transmit and receive BPDUs. This exchange is crucial because it allows the switch to continue participating in the spanning tree recalculation process. The Listening state ensures that any superior information about the root bridge or topology changes is propagated throughout the network. The duration of this state is determined by the forward delay timer, which is typically set to fifteen seconds.

Following the Listening state, if the port is still considered eligible for forwarding, it moves into the Learning state. This is where the port begins to populate the MAC address table based on incoming frames, learning which MAC addresses are reachable through this port. However, it still does not forward frames at this point. The Learning state is critical for preparing the switch to begin forwarding traffic without flooding the network. By the time the port transitions to Forwarding, it already has an idea of where certain devices reside within the network. Like the Listening state, the Learning state also typically lasts for fifteen seconds, depending on the forward delay timer setting.

Once a port has completed the Learning phase and the topology is confirmed to be loop-free, it enters the Forwarding state. In this state, the port forwards both user data and BPDUs. It fully participates in the network, allowing communication between devices and maintaining awareness of the topology. The Forwarding state represents the port's active and operational mode. It is the end goal for any port that is meant to carry traffic in a spanning tree-enabled network. However, if the network topology changes or if the port receives a superior BPDU indicating a better path to the root bridge exists elsewhere, it may revert to a previous state or even transition to the Blocking state once again.

A port may also enter the Disabled state, in which it does not participate in the spanning tree process at all. This could be due to administrative shutdown, physical disconnection, or an error condition. Unlike Blocking, Disabled ports do not listen for BPDUs and are essentially ignored by the STP algorithm. This state is not part of the active STP path selection process and is typically managed by administrative actions rather than protocol logic.

The sequence and timing of these port states serve a very specific purpose: to allow the network to converge gradually and safely without creating loops. In classic STP, the entire process of moving a port from Blocking to Forwarding can take up to thirty seconds. This delay was acceptable in earlier networks where stability was prioritized over speed, but in modern environments, it is often seen as a hindrance. For this reason, enhancements like Rapid Spanning Tree Protocol were introduced to accelerate port transitions. RSTP modifies how ports move between states and introduces new mechanisms such as proposal and agreement messages to reduce convergence time.

Despite the limitations in speed, the port state model in STP remains effective in preventing the catastrophic effects of Layer 2 loops. It provides a framework for switches to coordinate their behavior and respond methodically to changes in topology. For instance, if a primary link fails and a redundant link needs to become active, the previously blocked port must transition through Listening and Learning before it can begin Forwarding. This prevents sudden shifts that could destabilize the network or result in duplicated frames.

Understanding the implications of each port state also helps in diagnosing network issues. If a device suddenly loses connectivity, checking whether the associated switch port is stuck in Blocking or Learning can reveal whether the issue is due to STP convergence. Similarly, observing unexpected transitions can indicate problems with the spanning tree configuration, such as an unintentional change in the root bridge or incorrect port cost values.

The interaction of STP port states and their controlled transitions define the tempo of Ethernet Layer 2 resilience. While often happening behind the scenes, these transitions are the reason networks maintain connectivity even in the face of physical link failures or configuration changes. Each state plays a role in balancing the need for uptime with the requirement to prevent broadcast storms and maintain deterministic traffic paths. For network engineers and administrators, a clear understanding of these states is essential for optimizing performance, ensuring stability, and implementing effective monitoring and alerting in switched Ethernet environments.

The Root Bridge Election Process

The Root Bridge election process is a foundational mechanism within the Spanning Tree Protocol, serving as the initial and most critical step in building a loop-free Layer 2 topology. In any switched Ethernet network that utilizes STP, the root bridge acts as the logical center of the network. All path calculations are made with respect to this central reference point. Understanding how the root bridge is elected, what criteria are used during the selection, and how the result impacts the overall topology is essential for anyone working with STP-based network environments.

When switches in a network first come online, they begin exchanging Bridge Protocol Data Units, or BPDUs. These small frames carry information that includes the switch's bridge ID, which is a combination of a configurable priority value and the switch's MAC address. Initially, every switch considers itself to be the root bridge and sends BPDUs advertising its own bridge ID as the best. As these BPDUs are received by other switches, comparisons are made, and switches will stop advertising themselves as the root if they receive a superior BPDU, one that contains a bridge ID lower than their own. This process continues until all switches agree on a single root bridge, and all others relinquish their candidacy.

The root bridge election process hinges on two components of the bridge ID: the bridge priority and the MAC address. The bridge priority is a 16-bit value, with a default of 32768 on most switches. Network administrators can manually configure this value to influence the election process. The lower the priority value, the higher the chance that a switch will become the root bridge. If two switches have the same priority, the MAC address becomes the tiebreaker. In this case, the switch with the lower numerical MAC address is selected as the root. Because MAC addresses are supposed to be globally unique, this ensures that the election always produces a single result, even in networks with identical priority settings.

Once the root bridge is elected, it assumes a central role in the spanning tree topology. It continues to send BPDUs periodically, announcing itself as the root. These BPDUs are propagated throughout the network by other switches, which update their own path cost to the root bridge and determine which of their ports should be designated as forwarding or blocking. Each non-root switch identifies its best path to the root by calculating the cumulative cost of reaching the root through each of its ports. The port with the lowest path cost is selected as the root port and placed in the forwarding state. The remaining ports are evaluated for their role as designated ports for each network segment or blocked to prevent loops.

The choice of the root bridge has significant implications for the network topology and performance. Ideally, the root bridge should be placed in a central location within the network to minimize path costs and ensure balanced traffic flow. If the root bridge is elected randomly, the resulting topology may be inefficient, with suboptimal forwarding paths and underutilized high-speed links. Therefore, it is a common best practice for network administrators to manually configure bridge priority values to force the most suitable switch to become the root. This switch is typically a high-performance, well-connected core switch capable of handling the increased control plane traffic and serving as a stable anchor for the spanning tree.

In large networks, especially those using VLANs, the election process becomes more complex. Each VLAN runs its own instance of the Spanning Tree Protocol, meaning that there can be a different root bridge for each VLAN. In such scenarios, configuring the same switch as the root bridge for all VLANs may not be ideal. Instead, administrators often use per-VLAN root placement to optimize traffic flow for specific departments or services. This approach requires careful planning and configuration to ensure that spanning tree instances align with logical and physical network layouts.

The election process is not static. If the current root bridge fails or becomes unreachable due to a link or device failure, the switches detect the absence of BPDUs and begin a new election process. The remaining switches compare their bridge IDs using the same rules and agree on a new root. This dynamic re-election ensures that the spanning tree can self-heal and maintain a loop-free topology even in the face of failures. However, this convergence process can take time, especially in classic STP, which may result in temporary connectivity issues or degraded performance. Enhanced versions of STP, such as Rapid Spanning Tree Protocol, reduce this downtime by accelerating the re-election and re-convergence processes.

To monitor and control the root bridge election process, many switches offer commands to view the current root bridge, the received BPDUs, and the priority settings of connected devices. These tools are invaluable for troubleshooting network performance issues and verifying that the intended root bridge is in place. In environments with critical uptime requirements, administrators also use features like Root Guard to prevent unexpected devices from becoming the root bridge. This feature can be applied to specific ports where no superior BPDUs should ever be accepted, thus maintaining the integrity of the network design.

Problems can arise if two switches are configured with the same low priority value and both have low MAC addresses. This can result in an unintended switch becoming the root, potentially causing inefficient traffic patterns or topology instability. To avoid this, careful planning of bridge priorities across the network is essential. Additionally, in scenarios where virtualization or automated provisioning is used, care must be taken to ensure that newly introduced switches do not interfere with the existing spanning tree hierarchy.

The root bridge election process, while automatic and self-regulating, is not something that should be left to chance in a production environment. Proper configuration ensures that the most capable switch assumes the role of root bridge, supporting a stable and efficient Layer 2 topology. The decision impacts every subsequent calculation and forwarding decision made by other switches, influencing the entire behavior of the STP domain. By understanding the mechanics behind the election and how to influence it through configuration, network professionals can design and maintain predictable, resilient, and high-performing Ethernet networks.

Path Cost and Port Roles in STP

In the Spanning Tree Protocol, path cost and port roles are essential mechanisms used to determine how switches forward traffic and maintain a loop-free Layer 2 topology. These components work together to define the structure of the spanning tree and ensure that only the most efficient paths are used for forwarding, while redundant paths are blocked until needed. Understanding how STP calculates path cost and assigns port roles is vital to designing, maintaining, and troubleshooting reliable Ethernet networks.

Path cost is a numerical value assigned to each link in the network to represent the relative desirability of using that link as part of the active spanning tree. Lower path costs indicate more preferred paths. The cost is primarily based on the bandwidth of the link, with faster links assigned lower values. For example, a 10 Mbps link has a much higher cost than a 1 Gbps or 10 Gbps link. This cost-based calculation allows STP to favor high-speed links and avoid less efficient paths unless no better options are available. The original IEEE 802.1D standard used a simple cost table, but as link speeds increased, it became necessary to revise the calculation to accommodate gigabit and multi-gigabit connections without assigning a cost of zero. The revised STP cost formula uses 200,000,000 divided by the link speed in bits per second, resulting in lower costs for higher-speed links while maintaining granularity for large and complex topologies.

Each switch in the spanning tree calculates the total path cost to reach the root bridge. This total is the sum of the individual link costs along the path from the switch to the root. The switch then identifies the port that provides the lowest cumulative path cost and designates it as the root port. The root port is the switch's best path to the root bridge and is always placed in the forwarding state. Every non-root switch has exactly one root port, and this port forms the backbone of the spanning tree by ensuring that traffic flows efficiently toward the logical center of the network.

While the root port is critical for connecting non-root switches to the root bridge, the network must also manage traffic on segments that connect multiple switches. On each segment, one switch is chosen to forward frames onto the segment. This is where the designated port role comes into play. The designated port is the port on the switch that has the lowest path cost to the root bridge among all switches on the segment. This port is also placed in the forwarding state. All other ports on the segment that are not selected as designated ports or root ports are placed into the blocking state to prevent loops. Designated ports are responsible for forwarding traffic from their segments toward the root bridge, and they also handle BPDU transmission to maintain the topology.

A port that is neither a root port nor a designated port becomes a non-designated port and is placed in the blocking state. Blocking ports do not forward data frames or learn MAC addresses. Their only function is to listen for BPDUs and remain ready to transition into a forwarding role if the network topology changes. These ports provide the redundancy that gives STP its fault-tolerant properties. If a forwarding port or a link fails, STP recalculates the spanning tree, and a previously blocked port may be promoted to a forwarding role, restoring connectivity.

In more advanced implementations such as Rapid Spanning Tree Protocol, additional port roles are defined to accelerate convergence and provide more granular control. However, in classic STP, the three key roles—root port, designated port, and non-designated (blocking) port—remain central to how the protocol manages the flow of traffic and ensures loop prevention. The efficiency and stability of the entire network depend on accurate path cost calculations and correct port role assignments.

Path cost manipulation is a powerful tool in the hands of network engineers. By manually configuring the cost of certain ports, administrators can influence the spanning tree topology to match their design goals. For example, a network engineer might increase the cost of a slower backup link to ensure that it is only used if the faster primary link fails. This kind of tuning allows the network to reflect real-world constraints and performance expectations, avoiding scenarios where suboptimal links are inadvertently placed into forwarding states.

Port roles also influence the direction of traffic and the placement of load across the network. If all switches default to using the same root bridge and do not adjust their port costs, the resulting topology may create bottlenecks or underutilized links. By balancing the root bridge placement with adjusted port costs, engineers can create more symmetrical traffic patterns and improve overall efficiency. This is especially important in large-scale environments or where VLANs are distributed across multiple switches.

Understanding the dynamics of path cost and port roles is also critical when troubleshooting STP-related issues. Unexpected blocking or forwarding behavior can often be traced back to incorrect cost values or a misunderstood port role assignment. Tools that allow visibility into the spanning tree—such as commands to display current port roles and path costs—are invaluable for diagnosing and resolving these problems. Network documentation and topology maps become even more effective when port roles and cost configurations are clearly defined and maintained.

In virtualized or dynamic environments where physical topologies change frequently, STP continues to rely on accurate path cost metrics and port roles to maintain a stable network. As new links are introduced, switches must recalculate their paths and reassign port roles accordingly. Even in modern networks that use advanced alternatives like TRILL or SPB, the foundational concepts of path cost and port roles are retained in modified forms, reflecting their fundamental importance to loop prevention and topology control.

Ultimately, path cost and port roles are not merely configuration options—they are the mechanisms by which STP interprets and manages the physical topology of the network. Through precise calculation and consistent application, they allow Ethernet networks to support redundancy without loops, adapt to changes in real time, and optimize traffic flow across varied link types and speeds. Mastery of these principles is key to deploying scalable and resilient Layer 2 infrastructures.

Convergence in Legacy STP

Convergence in legacy Spanning Tree Protocol represents one of the most critical and historically limiting aspects of Layer 2 network design. In the context of networking, convergence refers to the process by which all switches in a spanning tree-enabled network agree on a loop-free topology after a change, such as the failure of a link or switch, the introduction of a new device, or a topology modification. In legacy STP, defined by the IEEE 802.1D standard, this convergence process was deliberately cautious and slow by modern standards, prioritizing stability and loop avoidance over speed. Although this method was effective in small or relatively static networks, it posed significant challenges as networks grew in size and complexity, and as business demands began to require high availability and rapid recovery.

The convergence process in legacy STP begins with the exchange of Bridge Protocol Data Units between switches. When a network starts up or when a topology change is detected, each switch initially assumes it is the root bridge and begins sending BPDUs advertising itself as such. These BPDUs include the bridge ID and path cost to the root. As switches receive BPDUs from their neighbors, they compare them to their current information and update their view of the network if a superior BPDU is received. Eventually, all switches agree on a single root bridge, and each non-root switch selects its root port—the port that offers the lowest cost path to the root bridge.

After determining the root port, switches identify which of their other ports will act as designated ports for each network segment and which will enter the blocking state to prevent loops. Only one designated port per segment is allowed to forward frames, and the port is chosen based on the lowest path cost to the root. All other ports are blocked. This process ensures that a single, loop-free tree is formed, with traffic flowing up to and down from the root bridge in a hierarchical manner.

The key limitation in legacy STP convergence lies in the time it takes for a port to transition from a blocking state to a forwarding state. When a link fails and STP recalculates the topology, the new path must go through a series of port states: blocking, listening, learning, and finally forwarding. Each of these states is governed by timers. The default timer values are two seconds for Hello Time, twenty seconds for Max Age, and fifteen seconds each for Listening and Learning states. These timers introduce a delay that can result in convergence times of up to fifty seconds or more under default configurations. During this time, affected segments of the network may be unreachable, causing application disruptions and potentially triggering failover mechanisms in higher layers of the network stack.

The design of these timers reflects the conservative nature of legacy STP. In the early days of Ethernet networking, stability and loop prevention were paramount. Because Ethernet frames do not have a time-to-live field like IP packets, a loop could cause frames to circulate indefinitely, consuming bandwidth and overwhelming devices. To avoid even the slightest risk of this occurring, STP was designed to wait and observe the network before transitioning ports to forwarding mode. The protocol waits to ensure that no superior BPDUs will arrive, that the topology is stable, and that MAC address tables can be safely rebuilt without causing misdirected traffic.

This cautious approach, however, became increasingly problematic in modern networks. The delay introduced by legacy STP convergence could not be tolerated in environments where applications require near-instantaneous availability. Voice over IP, video conferencing, real-time data replication, and other latency-sensitive services demand high-speed failover and recovery. As a result, legacy STP began to show its age, particularly in large enterprise networks or data centers with complex topologies and high redundancy.

One of the workarounds used to minimize the impact of slow convergence was to configure port features like PortFast on access ports. PortFast allows a port to skip the Listening and Learning states and immediately transition to forwarding, under the assumption that the device connected to the port is an end host, not another switch. While this helps end devices come online more quickly, it does not solve the core issue of long convergence times for switch-to-switch links or redundant paths within the core of the network. Additionally, if PortFast is misconfigured on ports connected to other switches, it can introduce serious stability issues by allowing loops to form before STP can react.

Network engineers would also sometimes manipulate bridge priorities and port costs manually to influence the topology in a way that minimized the need for recalculation. By carefully selecting the root bridge and preferred paths, administrators could reduce the likelihood of topology changes and thus limit convergence events. However, this required a deep understanding of the network's behavior and introduced configuration complexity that was difficult to maintain as networks scaled.

The limitations of convergence in legacy STP eventually led to the development of enhancements such as Rapid Spanning Tree Protocol, which dramatically reduced convergence time by eliminating the need for ports to pass through every intermediate state. RSTP introduced new mechanisms for port role negotiation and immediate transitions under safe conditions. It also allowed for the reuse of existing links without needing to wait for timers to expire, making it more suitable for the demands of contemporary networking.

Despite its drawbacks, legacy STP played a critical role in the evolution of Ethernet networking. It provided a reliable and deterministic method for preventing loops, enabling the use of redundant links without fear of broadcast storms or MAC table instability. Its design principles continue to influence modern networking technologies, and a foundational understanding of its convergence behavior remains important for troubleshooting, legacy support, and historical context. Even as newer protocols supplant it in production environments, the lessons learned from the convergence mechanisms of legacy STP continue to shape the design of resilient and adaptable network architectures.

STP Timers and Optimization Techniques

The Spanning Tree Protocol relies on a set of timers to manage the convergence process and ensure a stable, loop-free topology in Layer 2 networks. These timers determine how quickly the protocol reacts to topology changes, how long it waits before considering a path change, and how long it takes for a port to transition from one state to another. While the default timer values were chosen to prioritize network stability, they can introduce significant delays in environments that require fast failover and high availability. A deep understanding of STP timers and the techniques used to optimize them is essential for designing networks that are both resilient and responsive.

The three primary timers used by STP are the Hello Time, Forward Delay, and Max Age timers. Each one plays a specific role in controlling how BPDUs are exchanged and how ports transition between states. The Hello Time determines how frequently the root bridge sends BPDUs to all other switches in the network. By default, this interval is set to two seconds. The Forward Delay timer controls how long a port remains in the Listening and Learning states before it can enter the Forwarding state. Its default value is fifteen seconds, which results in a total of thirty seconds before a port can forward traffic after a topology change. The Max Age timer dictates how long a switch will wait without receiving a BPDU before it considers the information stale and begins recalculating the spanning tree. The default Max Age is twenty seconds.

Together, these timers define the overall responsiveness of the STP process. For example, when a topology change occurs, such as a link failure or the loss of a switch, it may take up to twenty seconds before the Max Age timer expires, followed by another thirty seconds for the affected ports to transition through the Listening and Learning states. This leads to a total potential convergence time of fifty seconds, which is often unacceptable in modern networks where critical services depend on continuous connectivity. The slow convergence has driven many organizations to either modify the default timer settings or implement optimization techniques that enhance STP responsiveness without compromising stability.

One of the most common techniques for improving STP performance is adjusting the Hello Time, Max Age, and Forward Delay values manually. By reducing the Hello Time, the root bridge sends BPDUs more frequently, allowing downstream switches to detect topology changes sooner. However, lowering this value too aggressively can increase CPU utilization on switches and lead to unnecessary recalculations. Reducing the Forward Delay can also speed up port transitions, but this must be done cautiously, as it increases the risk of loops forming if the topology has not fully stabilized. Adjusting the Max Age timer to a smaller value can also reduce downtime by enabling switches to detect the absence of BPDUs more quickly. When these timers are modified, they must remain within a valid range and maintain a logical relationship. For example, the Max Age must be at least two seconds greater than three times the Hello Time to ensure that switches have enough time to detect and process topology changes.

Another powerful technique for optimization involves the use of the PortFast feature. PortFast is designed for access ports that connect to end-user devices rather than other switches. When enabled, PortFast allows a port to bypass the Listening and Learning states and immediately enter the Forwarding state upon link-up. This drastically reduces the time it takes for devices like computers, printers, or phones to join the network. Since these devices do not participate in spanning tree calculations, enabling PortFast on such ports does not increase the risk of loops. However, if PortFast is mistakenly enabled on ports connected to other switches or bridging devices, it can cause temporary loops and broadcast storms before STP has a chance to react. Therefore, it should be used carefully and only in appropriate contexts.

BPDU Guard is often deployed alongside PortFast to prevent misconfigurations from introducing instability. If a PortFast-enabled port receives a BPDU, which indicates the presence of another switch, BPDU Guard disables the port to protect the network from unintended loops. This combination of PortFast and BPDU Guard not only accelerates convergence on access ports but also adds a layer of security and loop prevention, particularly in enterprise environments where unauthorized devices might be introduced to the network.

Another optimization technique involves tuning path cost values to influence spanning tree decisions. While not a timer in the strict sense, path cost indirectly affects convergence by guiding the selection of root ports and designated ports. By increasing the cost of backup links and lowering the cost of preferred links, network administrators can create a more deterministic topology that is less likely to require recalculation under normal operating conditions. This approach reduces the frequency of topology changes and minimizes the need for ports to go through state transitions, effectively improving the network's overall stability and responsiveness.

Rapid Spanning Tree Protocol represents a more advanced approach to optimization. It builds upon the limitations of traditional STP timers by introducing faster convergence mechanisms that eliminate the need for ports to remain in each intermediate state for a fixed duration. Instead of relying heavily on timers, RSTP uses a handshake process between switches to negotiate immediate forwarding decisions where it is safe to do so. Although RSTP still includes timers for backward compatibility and certain edge cases, it dramatically reduces convergence times, often to under a second. For environments where legacy STP is still in use, transitioning to RSTP offers the most effective optimization available and requires relatively minimal configuration changes.

Even in legacy STP deployments, careful planning and the use of features like UplinkFast and BackboneFast can improve convergence. UplinkFast accelerates the transition to a backup link when a directly connected uplink fails, while BackboneFast reduces the time required for indirect link failures to be detected and corrected. These features work by preemptively identifying alternative paths and adjusting timers or bypassing certain state transitions under controlled conditions.

Optimizing STP timers requires a balance between speed and reliability. Setting values too aggressively can lead to instability, unnecessary recalculations, and even loops if the network is not carefully monitored. Conversely, leaving all timer values at their defaults may result in sluggish convergence that fails to meet the performance demands of modern applications. Effective STP tuning begins with a thorough understanding of the network's topology, traffic patterns, and business requirements. By combining timer adjustments with other optimization techniques and implementing enhanced STP variants where possible, network engineers can build Layer 2 environments that respond quickly to change, minimize disruption, and maintain the resilience required in today's connected world.

Common STP Topologies and Pitfalls

Designing effective network topologies using the Spanning Tree Protocol requires a deep understanding of how STP operates and how different layouts impact performance, redundancy, and stability. The topology of a network determines how switches are interconnected and how traffic flows across the infrastructure. While STP provides loop prevention and automatic path selection, the way devices are arranged can influence the efficiency of the protocol and expose the network to certain pitfalls. Commonly used STP topologies each offer their own advantages, but they also carry specific risks and design flaws that must be carefully managed to avoid outages or degraded performance.

One of the most basic and frequently deployed STP topologies is the classic access-distribution-core model. In this architecture, access layer switches connect end-user devices and aggregate upstream to distribution layer switches. The distribution switches then connect to the core, where high-speed backbone links reside. STP is typically used to block redundant links between access switches and the distribution layer to prevent loops. In this model, the root bridge is usually placed in the distribution or core layer, depending on the size and function of the network. This hierarchical layout supports scalable growth and easy troubleshooting, but it relies heavily on careful placement of the root bridge and correct path cost tuning. A common pitfall in this topology is the unintentional election of an access switch as the root bridge due to default priority settings, which can cause suboptimal traffic flow and inefficient utilization of high-speed uplinks.

Another common topology is the dual-homed access layer, where each access switch is connected to two distribution switches for redundancy. This design enhances fault tolerance and ensures that end-user connectivity is not lost if a distribution switch fails. However, it introduces potential loops that must be blocked by STP. In many cases, one of the uplinks from each access switch is placed in a blocking state, meaning that only half of the available bandwidth is used under normal conditions. A frequent mistake in this configuration is failing to align STP root bridge placement with the active default gateway location, especially in networks using protocols like HSRP or VRRP. When traffic flows one way to reach the gateway and takes a different path to return due to spanning tree decisions, the result is suboptimal routing and unnecessary latency.

Ring topologies are also commonly seen in smaller networks, such as those used in industrial environments or small branch offices. A ring topology provides redundancy by connecting switches in a loop, which allows traffic to continue flowing in one direction if a segment fails. However, this topology relies heavily on STP to block one of the links to prevent a loop. When STP is slow to converge after a failure, the entire ring can become unresponsive. Additionally, if a link fails and then rapidly comes back online, flapping can occur, causing repeated recalculations of the spanning tree and network instability. To mitigate this, it is essential to use optimized STP versions such as Rapid STP or enable features like loop guard and port fast where appropriate.

Mesh topologies, particularly partial meshes, are sometimes used in data centers or environments requiring high redundancy and multiple paths. In this arrangement, each switch has several connections to multiple peers. While this provides excellent failover capabilities, it can also lead to a large number of blocked ports, as STP must prune most redundant links to maintain a loop-free topology. One of the most overlooked pitfalls in mesh topologies is the potential for inconsistent path cost calculations when bandwidth mismatches exist across links. For example, a gigabit uplink may be blocked in favor of a slower fast Ethernet link if STP path costs are not adjusted manually.

Misunderstanding how the STP algorithm evaluates cost can lead to unpredictable forwarding behavior and uneven traffic distribution.

Star topologies, where all switches connect to a central switch, are less common in enterprise environments due to limited scalability but still found in smaller or legacy networks. In this design, the central switch naturally becomes the root bridge and all other switches forward traffic to it. While this simplifies the STP topology and makes root bridge placement predictable, the central switch becomes a single point of failure. If this switch goes down, the entire network collapses, despite STP being in place. STP does not inherently provide protection from hardware failure of the root bridge; it only recalculates the topology after the failure is detected, which introduces downtime. A common pitfall here is assuming STP itself provides high availability without additional physical or logical redundancy.

In all topologies, another critical and often underestimated issue is the presence of unintentional loops caused by user error. Plugging a cable between two switch ports or enabling bridging features on end-user devices can introduce unexpected paths that STP was not designed to handle. Without protections like BPDU Guard, Root Guard, and Loop Guard, these issues can go undetected until they cause broadcast storms or severe disruptions. In networks where STP is not strictly enforced on all ports, or where certain segments are considered "safe" and left unguarded, accidental or malicious loops can still bring down the entire network.

Mismatched STP configurations between vendor platforms or different STP versions on adjacent switches can also create unpredictable behaviors. For example, legacy STP does not interact efficiently with Rapid STP unless properly configured for compatibility. BPDUs may be misinterpreted or ignored, causing ports to incorrectly stay in blocking or forwarding states. This can be especially problematic in networks undergoing gradual upgrades or those using a mix of old and new equipment.

The importance of accurate root bridge placement, consistent cost values, and proper STP feature implementation cannot be overstated in any topology. Poorly designed STP configurations can result in traffic congestion, asymmetric routing, long convergence times, or complete loss of connectivity. Thorough documentation, regular validation of topology behavior, and active monitoring of BPDU activity are essential practices for maintaining STP health across all types of network layouts.

Each common STP topology provides a balance between performance, redundancy, and complexity. The choice of topology should reflect the goals of the network design, the criticality of services, and the need for scalability. Avoiding the common pitfalls requires not only technical knowledge of the protocol but also a proactive approach to network management, where spanning tree behavior is tested, verified, and continuously aligned with the intended architecture. Only then can the full benefits of STP be realized without exposing the network to unnecessary risks.

STP Limitations in Modern Networks

The Spanning Tree Protocol was originally developed to solve a critical problem in early Ethernet networks: the risk of Layer 2 loops caused by redundant paths. While STP succeeded in this goal, the design and operational model of the protocol were built around the constraints and expectations of legacy environments. As network demands have evolved, especially with the rise of virtualization, cloud computing, real-time applications, and dense data center architectures, the limitations of STP have become more pronounced. These constraints have led to a re-evaluation of how Layer 2 redundancy and loop prevention should be implemented in modern networks.

One of the most significant limitations of STP in contemporary environments is its inherently slow convergence time. In traditional 802.1D STP, convergence after a topology change can take up to 50 seconds, factoring in the Max Age, Listening, and Learning timer durations. This delay is unacceptable in networks that host latency-sensitive services such as voice over IP, streaming media, or online transaction systems. Although enhancements like Rapid Spanning Tree Protocol reduce convergence times dramatically, the fundamental STP model still relies on a reactive approach, where ports wait for timer expirations before transitioning states. This reactive nature delays the full restoration of connectivity and can lead to service interruptions that are difficult to diagnose.

Another major drawback of STP is its inefficient use of network links. To prevent loops, STP blocks redundant paths, even if those links are physically available and fully operational. This leads to a topology where only a subset of the potential bandwidth is utilized at any given time. In environments where high availability and full link utilization are required, such as multi-homed data center fabrics or high-throughput enterprise backbones, this underutilization results in wasted capacity. Load balancing across redundant paths is not possible with traditional STP because it selects only one active path, relegating the others to standby roles until a failure occurs. This approach conflicts with the expectations of modern networking, where applications demand both high availability and maximum performance simultaneously.

STP also lacks any form of intelligent traffic engineering. It does not consider real-time link utilization, latency, or congestion when determining the best path to the root bridge. The path selection is purely based on predefined port costs, which are static unless manually adjusted. As a result, STP can select a technically shortest path that might be congested or operating suboptimally, while longer but less congested paths remain unused. This simplistic decision-making model cannot meet the demands of dynamic traffic patterns found in modern environments, where virtual machines migrate between hosts, and applications scale up and down in response to user demand.

Scalability is another area where STP shows its age. In large Layer 2 networks with hundreds or thousands of switches, STP can struggle to maintain a stable topology. The constant exchange of BPDUs, the recalculation of tree structures, and the risk of loops or misconfigurations increase with scale. Moreover, each VLAN in classic per-VLAN STP requires its own spanning tree instance, which significantly burdens CPU and memory resources on switches. While technologies like Multiple Spanning Tree Protocol attempt to address this by allowing multiple VLANs to share a single instance, the overall complexity of STP-based management grows rapidly in proportion to the size of the network.

Another limitation lies in STP's lack of flexibility and visibility in virtualized environments. As virtualization has become ubiquitous, virtual switches operating inside hypervisors have introduced new challenges to traditional Layer 2 designs. These virtual switches may form their own topologies, often invisible to the physical STP process. If not properly integrated, virtual machines can introduce loops, spoof BPDUs, or disrupt the expected behavior of the STP topology. The lack of direct STP integration with virtual infrastructure makes it more difficult to ensure consistency between physical and virtual Layer 2 domains. Furthermore, automation and orchestration tools used in modern cloud environments often expect near-instantaneous changes to network topology, something STP was never designed to support.

Security is another concern that becomes more significant in modern, open networks. STP assumes a cooperative and trusted environment. It does not include robust mechanisms to authenticate BPDUs or validate the identity of participating switches. As a result, an attacker who gains access to a network port can send superior BPDUs to claim root bridge status, altering the network topology and potentially redirecting traffic through malicious paths. While features such as BPDU Guard and Root Guard offer some protection, they require manual configuration and ongoing maintenance, increasing administrative overhead in large-scale deployments.

Troubleshooting STP-related issues in a modern network can also be difficult and time-consuming. Because STP decisions are made based on real-time BPDU analysis and relative path costs, diagnosing why a port is blocked or why traffic is taking a certain path requires examining the entire tree structure and the role of every port. As the size of the network grows, and as redundancy becomes more complex, this becomes a non-trivial task. Logs and monitoring tools may not provide enough context to easily identify the root cause of an issue, especially in environments where changes happen frequently and are sometimes automated through scripts or controllers.

In light of these limitations, many modern networks are shifting away from STP as the primary loop prevention and redundancy mechanism. Technologies such as TRILL, SPB, and EVPN offer alternative solutions that support full path utilization, faster convergence, and better integration with Layer 3 routing. These protocols replace the blocking and recalculation model of STP with link-state routing and encapsulation strategies that allow for multipath forwarding and active-active connections. In data centers, fabric technologies like VXLAN with EVPN overlays provide the scale, flexibility, and automation capabilities needed to meet modern application demands.

Despite these advancements, STP still persists in many networks due to its simplicity, widespread support, and ease of initial deployment. For smaller networks or those with relatively static topologies, STP continues to provide a functional and cost-effective solution. However, its role is increasingly being relegated to edge cases or legacy segments, as modern architectures adopt more agile and intelligent designs.

Recognizing the limitations of STP in today's fast-paced, high-performance networking world is essential for any engineer or architect tasked with building resilient infrastructure. While STP laid the groundwork for loop prevention and redundancy, the demands of modern networks have surpassed its capabilities. As organizations scale and adapt to digital transformation, the protocols that manage Layer 2 topologies must evolve as well, and relying solely on STP may no longer be sufficient to meet operational goals. The move toward more advanced, scalable, and application-aware network designs marks a necessary progression beyond the constraints imposed by traditional spanning tree implementations.

Rapid Spanning Tree Protocol Overview

Rapid Spanning Tree Protocol, standardized as IEEE 802.1w, was introduced as an enhancement to the original Spanning Tree Protocol to address the critical limitations in convergence time and network responsiveness. While legacy STP provided an effective solution to prevent Layer 2 loops, its slow convergence often proved to be a bottleneck in modern networks where uptime, performance, and resiliency are crucial. RSTP retains the core objective of maintaining a loop-free topology in bridged Ethernet networks but redefines the mechanisms by which switches communicate, negotiate topology changes, and transition ports between operational states.

RSTP is designed to be backward compatible with classic 802.1D STP, allowing it to function in networks where both protocols coexist. This compatibility was a key design decision to ease the adoption of RSTP in existing infrastructures. However, when all switches in a network support and operate in RSTP mode, the full benefits of its improvements are realized. One of the primary advantages of RSTP is its ability to significantly reduce the time it takes for the network to recover from a failure. Where legacy STP could take upwards of fifty seconds to respond to a topology change, RSTP can typically converge in less than a second under optimal conditions.

The most substantial improvement in RSTP lies in its port state and role model. While STP uses five port states—blocking, listening, learning, forwarding, and disabled—RSTP simplifies the model by eliminating the listening state and streamlining the transition process. Ports in RSTP operate in only three states: discarding, learning, and forwarding. This simplification reduces the time a port must wait before becoming operational, contributing to faster convergence. The discarding state encompasses both the legacy blocking and listening behaviors, preventing data traffic from being forwarded while still allowing BPDUs to be received and processed.

In addition to simplified states, RSTP introduces new port roles that better reflect the dynamic nature of modern networks. These roles include root port, designated port, and alternate or backup port. The root port is the same as in STP—it represents the best path from a non-root switch to the root bridge. The designated port is the forwarding port for a given segment, ensuring traffic can reach the root bridge. The alternate port is a new role that represents a backup path to the root bridge in case the primary root port fails. Similarly, the backup port provides a redundant path on a shared media segment, such as when multiple ports on the same switch connect to the same collision domain. These additional roles allow RSTP to pre-select alternate paths and enable immediate transitions if the active path fails, eliminating the need to wait for timer expirations.

Another major difference between RSTP and traditional STP is the manner in which topology changes are handled. In legacy STP, a topology change would trigger the transmission of topology change notifications, and the entire network would react by aging out MAC address entries after a short interval. This could lead to widespread disruption as devices were forced to relearn MAC addresses. RSTP improves this process by localizing the effect of topology changes. Only ports that are directly affected by the change react by flushing MAC address entries, preserving network stability and reducing the impact of routine events like port up/down changes or link failures.

RSTP also improves the way switches interact and negotiate their roles within the topology. It introduces a proposal and agreement mechanism that accelerates the convergence of point-to-point links. When a new link comes online, one switch proposes its role to the peer device. If the peer agrees and confirms that the path is valid and does not introduce loops, it responds with an agreement, and both ports can transition directly to the forwarding state. This bidirectional handshake removes the need for forward delay timers and reduces the reliance on passive observation of BPDUs. In cases where the link is not point-to-point, such as those involving shared media like hubs, RSTP reverts to slower mechanisms to maintain compatibility and reliability.

One of the practical benefits of RSTP is its ability to recover quickly from common failure scenarios without human intervention. For example, in a topology where a switch has two uplinks to redundant distribution switches, RSTP can maintain one path in the alternate role. If the active link fails, the alternate port can be immediately transitioned to the forwarding state without waiting for Max Age or forward delay timers. This rapid failover capability is especially important in enterprise and data center environments, where downtime is costly and application performance is sensitive to even brief disruptions.

Despite these enhancements, RSTP still operates within the constraints of a tree-based topology. It cannot leverage multiple active paths for load balancing across redundant links. Unlike more advanced Layer 2 technologies such as TRILL or SPB, RSTP continues to block some links to prevent loops, meaning that full bandwidth utilization across redundant paths remains unachievable. Nonetheless, its significantly faster recovery and greater operational efficiency make it a substantial improvement over traditional STP for networks that continue to rely on Layer 2 redundancy.

Implementing RSTP typically requires minimal configuration. Most modern switches support it natively and can be configured to operate in RSTP mode with a single command. When RSTP is enabled, the switch begins using the new protocol to generate and process BPDUs, and it automatically detects whether neighboring switches support RSTP or only legacy STP. In mixed environments, RSTP reverts to STP behavior to maintain interoperability. To achieve the best results, all switches in the spanning tree domain should support and run RSTP, enabling the network to fully benefit from the enhanced convergence capabilities.

RSTP also supports optional features such as port edge behavior, which is similar to STP's PortFast. Edge ports, which connect to end devices rather than other switches, can immediately transition to the forwarding state without any negotiation or delay. This ensures that hosts can join the network quickly without waiting for the protocol to evaluate the link. BPDU Guard can be applied to edge ports to protect against accidental or malicious connection of switches, which could otherwise interfere with the topology and create instability.

In the broader context of networking, RSTP represents a logical evolution of the spanning tree concept. It recognizes the growing need for rapid adaptation to change and more resilient behavior in complex topologies. By introducing improved state management, proactive path selection, and bidirectional negotiation, RSTP addresses the fundamental weaknesses of its predecessor while maintaining compatibility and simplicity. For organizations that need fast convergence but are not yet ready to adopt fully routed or fabric-based topologies, RSTP offers a reliable and efficient bridge between legacy design and modern performance expectations.

Comparing RSTP and Legacy STP

The evolution from the original Spanning Tree Protocol to Rapid Spanning Tree Protocol marks a significant step in the development of Layer 2 loop prevention mechanisms. Both protocols share the same fundamental goal of preventing broadcast storms and network loops in Ethernet networks with redundant paths, but they differ substantially in their methods, efficiency, and convergence behavior. A clear understanding of the differences between RSTP and legacy STP is critical for designing and managing networks that require high availability, fast failover, and modern scalability.

Legacy STP, defined by IEEE 802.1D, was designed in an era when networks were relatively simple and the need for redundancy was limited. Its process for achieving loop-free topologies relies on a slow, timer-based convergence model. When a topology change is detected, STP triggers a series of state transitions that must be completed before traffic can resume on the affected path. Each port moves through a strict sequence: starting in blocking, then progressing through listening, learning, and finally forwarding. The duration of each state is controlled by fixed timers—Forward Delay, Max Age, and Hello Time. Under default configurations, it can take up to fifty seconds for a port to move from blocking to forwarding following a topology change. During this time, segments of the network may be unreachable, and services relying on network connectivity can experience interruptions.

RSTP, standardized as IEEE 802.1w, addresses the primary drawback of legacy STP by drastically reducing convergence times. Rather than relying on timers to drive state transitions, RSTP introduces a handshake mechanism that allows switches to negotiate forwarding decisions dynamically and almost immediately. Ports in RSTP are no longer forced to wait for predefined intervals unless absolutely necessary. Instead, they can transition to forwarding state within milliseconds if the network conditions allow. This capability transforms the recovery behavior of the protocol, enabling networks to maintain near-continuous connectivity even during link failures or reconfigurations.

Another key area of differentiation is the port state model. Legacy STP uses five port states—blocking, listening, learning, forwarding, and disabled. These states describe the progression of a port during the process of joining or leaving the active topology. In contrast, RSTP simplifies the model by using only three port states: discarding, learning, and forwarding. The discarding state combines the functionality of both the blocking and listening states from legacy STP, reducing the number of transitional phases and making the behavior more predictable and efficient. Fewer states also mean fewer transitions and less delay, contributing to RSTP's superior performance in environments where uptime is critical.

RSTP also introduces a refined concept of port roles. While both protocols use root ports and designated ports to establish the loop-free path to the root bridge, RSTP adds alternate and backup port roles. An alternate port is a redundant path to the root bridge, maintained in a discarding state but immediately available if the primary root port fails. A backup port is similar but exists on the same collision domain, such as in a hub-based environment. These additional roles give RSTP the ability to preemptively identify alternate paths and activate them instantly when necessary, further contributing to rapid convergence and network resilience.

Topology change handling also sees a significant improvement in RSTP. In legacy STP, a topology change triggers the generation of topology change notifications, which are flooded throughout the network. These notifications cause all switches to shorten their MAC address aging timers, forcing a relearning of the network. This global response often results in unnecessary flooding and disrupted traffic even when the change affects only a small portion of the network. RSTP localizes the impact of topology changes. When a port transitions to forwarding or learning, it only affects the MAC address table on the local switch, avoiding widespread disruption and unnecessary flushing of forwarding tables across the entire topology.

Interoperability is another critical area where RSTP and STP differ. RSTP is designed to be backward compatible with STP. When an RSTP-enabled switch detects that its peer is running legacy STP, it reverts to 802.1D behavior for that link. This ensures that mixed environments can function without creating instability, though it also means that the advantages of RSTP are diminished on links where legacy STP is still in use. Full benefits of RSTP can only be realized when all switches in the network operate in RSTP mode.

From a configuration and deployment standpoint, RSTP is typically easier to manage than legacy STP. Modern switches support RSTP natively, and enabling it usually involves a simple configuration change. Once enabled, the switch automatically adjusts its behavior based on the capabilities of neighboring devices. RSTP also reduces the reliance on manual tuning of timers, as its faster convergence model is more tolerant of default settings. In contrast, optimizing legacy STP often requires manual adjustment of timer values and careful tuning of bridge priorities and port costs to ensure the desired topology is formed and maintained.

Despite its many advantages, RSTP retains certain design principles from STP that can still limit network performance. Like STP, it maintains a single active path between any two network segments, with all other redundant links placed in a discarding state. This means that, although RSTP provides fast failover, it still does not utilize all available bandwidth for active forwarding. Networks with high demands for link utilization and load balancing may find this model restrictive, prompting the need for more advanced technologies like TRILL or Shortest Path Bridging that support multipath forwarding.

One of the most telling differences between RSTP and legacy STP lies in how each protocol views the network. Legacy STP is entirely reactive, waiting for timers to expire and for BPDUs to arrive before making decisions. RSTP, by contrast, is more proactive, using immediate negotiation and predefined backup paths to ensure rapid response. This difference in approach reflects the changing requirements of network environments. As networks became faster and more complex, with applications requiring greater availability and responsiveness, the limitations of a purely timer-based protocol became increasingly problematic. RSTP emerged as the natural evolution, maintaining compatibility with the original design while addressing its most glaring deficiencies.

Ultimately, the comparison between RSTP and legacy STP highlights a transition in networking priorities. Where legacy STP prioritized cautious stability, RSTP brings speed and efficiency to the forefront without sacrificing reliability. It is not simply a faster version of its predecessor, but a redesigned protocol that embraces modern expectations for performance and resilience. For organizations still relying on traditional STP, the migration to RSTP represents a low-risk, high-reward improvement that can greatly enhance network responsiveness and reduce the operational impact of link and device failures. Understanding the distinctions between these protocols is essential for anyone responsible for designing, maintaining, or optimizing Ethernet networks in the current era.

Edge Ports and Link Types in RSTP

Rapid Spanning Tree Protocol introduces several enhancements over the original STP model, not only in terms of convergence speed but also in how it classifies and handles different types of links. One of the key features that contributes to RSTP's performance improvements is its ability to identify and treat ports differently based on their function and the type of connection they represent. Among the most important classifications are edge ports and link types. These distinctions enable RSTP to make faster and more intelligent forwarding decisions, optimizing the network's responsiveness while preserving its loop-free characteristics.

Edge ports are a concept unique to RSTP and were introduced to address a specific inefficiency in the original STP design. In a traditional STP environment, any port that becomes active must transition through the listening and learning states before it can begin forwarding traffic, even if it connects to a device that poses no risk of creating a loop. This process introduces unnecessary delays for end-user devices such as computers, printers, or IP phones, which typically do not participate in bridging and cannot cause loops. RSTP addresses this by allowing administrators to explicitly configure ports as edge ports. An edge port is one that connects directly to a single host device rather than another switch or bridge. When a port is marked as an edge port, RSTP immediately transitions it to the forwarding state as soon as the link becomes active, bypassing the traditional STP state transitions.

This immediate transition significantly reduces the time it takes for devices to gain network access, which is especially important in environments with dynamic endpoint connectivity or where rapid device boot times are expected. For instance, users plugging laptops into a network, or VoIP phones needing instant access to their call manager, benefit from the near-instantaneous connectivity provided by edge ports. From a technical standpoint, an edge port still participates in the BPDU exchange process to maintain consistency with the protocol but behaves differently when it comes to state transitions. If a BPDU is unexpectedly received on an edge port, indicating that a switch or bridging device has been connected instead of a host, RSTP will automatically remove the edge designation from the port and treat it as a regular port. This built-in safeguard prevents loops that could arise from misconfigurations or unauthorized equipment.

To enhance the safety of edge port configurations, network engineers often pair this feature with BPDU Guard. BPDU Guard is a protection mechanism that places a port into an err-disabled state if a BPDU is received. This is especially useful in enterprise environments where users might accidentally or maliciously connect a small switch or bridging device to an access port. By shutting down the port upon BPDU detection, the network prevents the introduction of unintended loops or disruptions to the established spanning tree. The combination of edge port functionality and BPDU Guard creates a secure and high-performance access layer that supports rapid convergence without compromising loop prevention.

In addition to edge ports, RSTP classifies point-to-point and shared links to further enhance the protocol's behavior based on the underlying medium. Point-to-point links refer to direct connections between two switches using full-duplex communication, such as Ethernet links without any intermediate hubs. These links are ideal for RSTP's proposal and agreement handshake mechanism, which is used to expedite the convergence process. When a switch detects a point-to-point link, it can rapidly negotiate port roles with its peer. This allows the port to move quickly into the forwarding state without waiting for timers to expire. The switch sends a proposal to the other side, suggesting its role in the topology. If the other switch agrees that the proposed topology is loop-free, it responds with an agreement message, and both sides can transition to forwarding immediately. This process drastically reduces convergence time compared to legacy STP's passive timer-based approach.

Shared links, on the other hand, are treated more conservatively. These links typically involve half-duplex communication or involve hubs where more than two devices may exist on the same collision domain.

Because the protocol cannot guarantee the same level of control and isolation as with point-to-point links, RSTP defaults to legacy STP behavior on shared links. This includes relying on traditional timers and slower state transitions to avoid loops. While shared links are less common in modern switched networks due to the obsolescence of hubs and half-duplex configurations, RSTP's ability to recognize and adapt to them ensures compatibility and safe operation in mixed or legacy environments.

Correct classification of link types is essential for ensuring optimal performance and stability in an RSTP-enabled network. Administrators can manually configure link types on some switches, while others automatically detect the nature of the connection based on duplex settings or link characteristics. In environments where auto-negotiation or improper cabling might confuse link type detection, manual configuration can help enforce predictable behavior. For example, setting a link to explicitly be treated as point-to-point ensures that rapid convergence mechanisms are used, even if the switch is unable to infer the link's characteristics correctly.

Understanding the role of edge ports and link types in RSTP is also crucial during network troubleshooting and maintenance. When a port does not behave as expected—such as taking longer than anticipated to begin forwarding—it is often due to misclassification. A port that should be an edge port might be missing its configuration, or a point-to-point link might be misdetected as shared due to mismatched duplex settings. Knowing how RSTP interprets these port types allows engineers to diagnose and correct issues more efficiently.

In larger topologies where redundancy is heavily utilized, the benefits of proper edge port configuration and accurate link type recognition are amplified. Networks that rely on fast convergence, especially those supporting virtualization, VoIP, or real-time applications, depend on the deterministic behavior provided by these features. The ability of RSTP to treat access ports and core interconnections differently reflects a more intelligent and context-aware approach to loop prevention and path optimization. Rather than enforcing a one-size-fits-all process, RSTP adapts its behavior based on the expected use of each link, enabling both speed and safety.

Ultimately, the introduction of edge ports and differentiated link types in RSTP represents a significant advancement over the original spanning tree protocol. These features allow network designers to construct more responsive, reliable, and scalable Layer 2 infrastructures while maintaining backward compatibility and operational safety. They demonstrate RSTP's awareness of modern networking realities, where endpoints demand immediate connectivity and core links must recover from failure without delay. Mastery of these concepts is essential for engineers seeking to leverage the full capabilities of RSTP and deliver robust, high-performance Ethernet networks.

RSTP Port Roles and State Machine

Rapid Spanning Tree Protocol enhances the foundational concepts of the original Spanning Tree Protocol by introducing a more refined and efficient approach to port roles and the state machine. These improvements are aimed at dramatically reducing convergence time and providing faster recovery from network topology changes, while maintaining a loop-free Layer 2 environment. Unlike traditional STP, which relied heavily on timers and a rigid progression of port states, RSTP implements a more dynamic model that emphasizes real-time negotiation and immediate role reassignment. This transformation is particularly evident in the way RSTP handles port roles and how it defines the behavior of each port through its simplified state machine.

At the heart of RSTP's operation are the port roles, which determine how each switch port participates in the forwarding of data and the propagation of BPDUs. RSTP recognizes five port roles: root port, designated port, alternate port, backup port, and disabled port. Each role is assigned based on the port's function within the network topology and its relative path to the root bridge. These roles are used by the RSTP algorithm to decide which ports will actively forward traffic and which will remain in standby or non-operational states to prevent loops.

The root port is the most important forwarding port on a non-root switch. It represents the shortest path, in terms of cost, from that switch to the root bridge. Only one root port exists per switch, and it is always in the forwarding state. The root port is the primary link through which the switch communicates with the rest of the network and maintains its role in the spanning tree. If the root port fails, RSTP quickly activates a backup path, usually through an alternate port, to maintain connectivity and avoid unnecessary disruption.

The designated port is the port on a network segment that is responsible for forwarding frames toward and from the root bridge. For each segment, there is one designated port, which resides on the switch that has the lowest path cost to the root bridge on that particular link. Like the root port, the designated port is placed in the forwarding state. It is responsible not only for passing traffic but also for sending BPDUs to maintain the stability and structure of the spanning tree.

Alternate ports are a new addition in RSTP that do not exist in the original STP model. These ports provide a backup path to the root bridge and are kept in a discarding state under normal conditions. What makes alternate ports powerful is their readiness to transition to forwarding immediately if the root port fails. Unlike legacy STP, which waits for timers to expire before activating new links, RSTP keeps alternate ports on standby and uses rapid agreement mechanisms to quickly promote them to active roles when needed.

Backup ports are similar in concept to alternate ports, but they exist on network segments with multiple connections to the same switch, such as when two ports on a switch are connected to the same shared medium. Backup ports are also in the discarding state and are used only if the designated port on the same segment becomes unavailable. These ports are rarely seen in modern full-duplex switched networks, but RSTP retains support for them for compatibility with older or hybrid configurations.

Disabled ports are those that are administratively shut down or otherwise unavailable for use by the spanning tree. They are not considered in any STP calculations and do not participate in BPDU exchanges. Disabled ports provide a way for administrators to manage and control network topology manually or to segment parts of the network that should not be part of the spanning tree domain.

The RSTP state machine is simplified compared to the original STP model, using only three states: discarding, learning, and forwarding. The discarding state encompasses the behavior of both blocking and listening states in STP. A port in the discarding state does not forward frames or learn MAC addresses. However, it still processes BPDUs, allowing it to monitor the topology and be ready to transition to another state when conditions allow. This simplification reduces the number of state transitions and enables faster decision-making within the protocol.

In the learning state, a port begins to populate the MAC address table with source addresses from incoming frames, but it still does not forward user data. This allows the switch to establish a reliable mapping of MAC addresses to ports before any data is forwarded. The learning state is short-lived, and its purpose is to ensure that, once the port transitions to forwarding, the switch already knows where to send frames, minimizing unnecessary flooding.

Finally, the forwarding state is the fully operational state in which the port actively forwards user traffic and BPDUs. This is the target state for any port that is part of the active spanning tree. The transition to forwarding is determined by the outcome of port role assignment and, in many cases, by the rapid handshake mechanism between switches. RSTP uses proposal and agreement messages to allow point-to-point links to skip the traditional delay and transition quickly to forwarding if no loops are detected.

This handshake mechanism is one of the most notable enhancements in RSTP. When a switch identifies a new point-to-point link, it can send a proposal BPDU to the peer switch. If the peer switch determines that enabling the port will not create a loop, it responds with an agreement message. This immediate exchange allows both ports to move to the forwarding state without relying on timers. This mechanism, combined with pre-assigned port roles like alternate and backup, enables RSTP to achieve convergence in under a second in most cases, a dramatic improvement over the lengthy convergence times in STP.

Understanding how RSTP assigns port roles and manages state transitions is critical to designing efficient and resilient Layer 2 topologies. Engineers must be able to anticipate how the protocol will respond to failures, new connections, or changes in link conditions. Properly identifying root ports, tuning path costs to influence designated port selection, and configuring edge and point-to-point links correctly all depend on a solid grasp of the RSTP port role and state machine model.

In practical deployments, visibility into RSTP's decisions is equally important. Most modern switches provide diagnostic commands that display current port roles, port states, and BPDU statistics. These insights help administrators verify that the spanning tree is behaving as expected and provide guidance when troubleshooting unexpected link behavior or performance issues. Because RSTP reacts dynamically to changes, monitoring tools must be able to reflect real-time state transitions and the rationale behind role reassignments.

By redefining the way ports are categorized and how they transition between operational modes, RSTP achieves a level of responsiveness and control that legacy STP could not offer. The combination of proactive role assignment, streamlined states, and rapid negotiation mechanisms forms a robust framework for maintaining network stability in environments that demand speed, reliability, and adaptability. These advancements make RSTP an essential component in modern network architectures, particularly in access, distribution, and aggregation layers where convergence speed is a critical factor.

Convergence Acceleration in RSTP

One of the most important innovations brought by Rapid Spanning Tree Protocol is its ability to dramatically accelerate convergence after a topology change. In traditional Spanning Tree Protocol, convergence was hindered by a dependency on fixed timers and a conservative approach that prioritized stability over responsiveness. The result was often lengthy network outages of up to fifty seconds during link failures or reconfigurations. This delay was unacceptable in environments requiring high availability and minimal service interruption. RSTP was designed specifically to overcome this limitation by introducing several mechanisms that allow switches to respond almost immediately to topology changes without compromising the loop-free integrity of the network.

At the heart of RSTP's fast convergence is the concept of a proactive, event-driven model. Unlike the passive behavior of legacy STP, where ports waited for timers to expire before transitioning between states, RSTP enables ports to make decisions based on real-time conditions and communication with neighboring switches. The state machine in RSTP is simplified, consisting only of three states: discarding, learning, and forwarding. By eliminating the listening state and merging it with discarding, RSTP removes one of the main sources of delay found in classic STP.

One of the most effective tools in accelerating convergence is the proposal and agreement mechanism used on point-to-point links. When a switch detects a new connection on a point-to-point interface, it sends a proposal message to its peer. This proposal indicates the intent to transition the port to the designated role and to begin forwarding traffic. If the neighboring switch determines that doing so will not introduce a loop, it responds with an agreement message. Once this exchange is completed, the ports can immediately enter the forwarding state without waiting for forward delay timers. This allows new links to become operational in a matter of milliseconds rather than waiting for seconds or tens of seconds under the older protocol. This rapid negotiation process works only on full-duplex, point-to-point connections, where the risk of loops is minimal and topology control is more straightforward.

Another key aspect of RSTP's convergence improvement is the introduction of alternate and backup port roles. These roles allow switches to maintain a ready-to-use secondary path to the root bridge without activating it until needed. An alternate port is one that provides an alternate path to the root bridge, typically found in topologies with redundant uplinks. A backup port is similar but exists on shared segments, such as those connected through legacy hubs. Both of these ports are in the discarding state under normal conditions but are constantly monitored by the switch. If the root port fails, the alternate port can be promoted to root port status and transitioned to the forwarding state immediately, bypassing the traditional waiting periods. This capability eliminates the need to wait for the Max Age timer to expire, as the switch already has a validated, pre-calculated path to the root.

Edge ports further contribute to faster convergence by allowing access ports connected to end devices to skip the typical progression through intermediate states. These ports are assumed to pose no risk of creating a loop and can therefore transition immediately to forwarding as soon as the link becomes active. This feature is especially valuable in environments with frequent user connections and disconnections, such as office networks or educational institutions. Devices connected to edge ports gain network access without delay, improving the user experience and minimizing disruptions caused by reboots or physical link changes. The use of BPDU Guard with edge ports ensures that if a switch or bridge is accidentally connected to such a port, it will be disabled immediately to prevent loops.

RSTP also improves the detection and handling of topology changes through its refined topology change notification mechanism. In classic STP, when a topology change occurred, the root bridge would generate topology change notifications that were flooded across the entire network. Each switch would then reduce its MAC address aging timer to a shorter interval, leading to widespread MAC table flushes. This approach could result in temporary flooding of unknown unicast traffic and inefficient use of bandwidth. RSTP limits the scope of topology changes to only those parts of the network that are directly affected. When a non-edge port transitions to the forwarding state, the switch informs its peers of the change, and only the affected switches adjust their MAC address tables. This targeted response reduces unnecessary disruption and keeps network traffic flowing smoothly.

In dynamic environments where links are frequently added, removed, or fail temporarily, RSTP's ability to respond quickly makes a substantial difference in maintaining service availability. The cumulative effect of the proposal-agreement process, the role of alternate and backup ports, the simplification of the port state machine, and localized topology change propagation creates a protocol that converges in real time. Under ideal conditions, RSTP can detect a link failure and restore full connectivity in under one second. This speed makes it possible to support real-time services such as voice, video, and critical data applications with minimal impact during network events.

Another benefit of RSTP's convergence model is its predictability. Because the protocol responds to events immediately and uses clearly defined roles and transitions, it behaves consistently across various topologies and implementations. Engineers can design networks with confidence that failover will occur within a tightly bounded time frame. This predictability is essential in environments with strict service-level agreements or in industries such as finance, healthcare, and manufacturing where downtime can lead to serious operational or financial consequences.

The rapid convergence offered by RSTP also enhances network resilience in distributed architectures. As organizations adopt more distributed applications and services, spanning multiple sites or data centers, the need for Layer 2 failover mechanisms that do not introduce delays becomes even more critical. RSTP fits well into these scenarios, allowing for highly available designs without the burden of long failover windows or complex timer tuning. It enables network topologies that are both redundant and responsive, minimizing the trade-off between reliability and speed.

Efficient convergence is not only about fast transitions but also about avoiding unnecessary reconvergence. RSTP achieves this by ensuring that ports only change state when needed, and by keeping alternate paths ready but inactive until they are required. This proactive design reduces the frequency and scope of recalculations, even in busy or high-change environments. The protocol's ability to isolate topology changes to affected segments, rather than propagate changes throughout the entire network, contributes to its overall stability and performance.

In real-world deployments, the benefits of RSTP's accelerated convergence are immediate and measurable. Network administrators report fewer user complaints during reboots or maintenance, improved uptime statistics, and smoother operation of critical services. When implemented correctly, RSTP provides a seamless experience during network transitions, aligning with modern expectations of always-on connectivity and continuous service delivery. This capability, combined with its backward compatibility and straightforward configuration, makes RSTP a powerful choice for both enterprise and service provider networks aiming to maintain robust, fast-reacting Layer 2 environments.

Backward Compatibility Considerations

When deploying Rapid Spanning Tree Protocol in existing networks, backward compatibility becomes a crucial consideration. Many enterprise environments are not built from scratch but evolve over time, incorporating legacy equipment alongside modern hardware. This often results in a mix of devices that support different versions of the Spanning Tree Protocol. Ensuring that these devices can coexist without introducing instability or service disruptions requires a comprehensive understanding of how RSTP interacts with the older 802.1D standard. The ability of RSTP to maintain compatibility with legacy STP was a key design goal and remains one of the protocol's most important features in real-world implementations.

The foundation of backward compatibility in RSTP lies in its ability to detect the protocol version being used by neighboring devices. When an RSTP-enabled switch receives a traditional 802.1D BPDU from a neighboring device, it automatically recognizes the need to fall back to legacy STP behavior for that specific port. This dynamic adjustment ensures that the switch does not attempt to engage in RSTP's faster negotiation mechanisms, which the legacy device would not understand. Instead, the RSTP switch reverts to using the legacy state transitions and timers, effectively emulating a classic STP environment on that port while still operating as RSTP elsewhere in the network.

This per-port compatibility model allows a network to gradually transition from legacy STP to RSTP without requiring an immediate and complete overhaul of all hardware. A network operator can enable RSTP on modern switches while still maintaining connectivity and stable operations with older switches that support only 802.1D. Over time, as older devices are replaced or upgraded, the number of legacy STP segments diminishes, and more of the network benefits from the rapid convergence features of RSTP. However, during the transition period, it is critical to understand that any link between an RSTP switch and an STP-only switch will behave according to legacy STP rules, including the full convergence delay imposed by the traditional timers.

Because RSTP must maintain compatibility on a per-port basis, the overall network convergence time will only be as fast as its slowest link. If a single switch in the topology supports only STP, it can become a bottleneck during topology changes, forcing other RSTP devices to wait for timer-based reconvergence. In designs where high availability and performance are priorities, it is important to identify these legacy devices and, if possible, isolate them from the main traffic paths. For example, legacy switches might be placed at the network edge where their impact on convergence is minimal, while core and distribution layers are upgraded to RSTP-compatible equipment.

Another key consideration in backward compatibility involves BPDU formatting. Legacy STP uses a specific BPDU format defined in 802.1D, while RSTP introduces a slightly different version for its own enhanced messages. When interoperating with STP devices, RSTP switches must send and accept the older BPDU format to ensure the legacy devices can interpret the messages correctly. This exchange prevents any loss of connectivity or miscommunication between switches operating on different protocols. However, it also means that RSTP's advanced features, such as proposal and agreement handshakes, alternate port roles, and rapid state transitions, are disabled on those links. The port essentially becomes a traditional STP port until the legacy neighbor is removed or upgraded.

Compatibility is not limited to technical protocol handling; it also involves configuration alignment. Some of the features commonly used in STP networks, such as PortFast, BPDU Guard, and root bridge priority settings, must be reviewed and adapted when integrating RSTP. For instance, while PortFast in STP simply allows a port to bypass listening and learning states, in RSTP, the equivalent functionality is provided by edge ports. Administrators must ensure that PortFast-configured ports are correctly converted to edge ports in RSTP to avoid unexpected behavior. Similarly, features like BPDU Guard continue to function as expected but must be validated against the updated RSTP behavior, particularly in environments where dynamic topology changes are common.

Mismatched configurations can also pose challenges in hybrid STP-RSTP environments. If one segment of the network uses customized STP timers and another segment runs RSTP with default values, inconsistencies can arise. For example, if the Hello Time on the STP side is modified to a non-standard value, it could lead to timing mismatches that affect BPDU interpretation or topology stability. To avoid such issues, it is recommended to standardize timer settings across the network or ensure that RSTP switches adjust their timing dynamically to accommodate legacy behavior. Many modern switches offer the ability to detect and adapt to these discrepancies automatically, but careful planning and documentation remain essential.

In multi-vendor networks, backward compatibility becomes even more complex due to slight differences in how various manufacturers implement STP and RSTP. Although the protocols are standardized, interpretations and default configurations can vary. Some vendors may use proprietary enhancements that are not compatible with standard RSTP behavior, leading to unexpected outcomes when connecting switches from different manufacturers. Thorough interoperability testing is required before deploying RSTP in such environments. Documentation from each vendor should be consulted to confirm how compatibility is handled and what adjustments might be needed to ensure stable operation.

During the migration phase from STP to RSTP, network monitoring becomes even more important. Administrators should use network management tools and command-line utilities to verify the status of each port, the protocol version being used, and the convergence behavior after topology changes. Logs and debug commands can reveal whether a port has fallen back to STP mode due to a legacy neighbor, allowing administrators to track and plan upgrades accordingly. Regular testing of failover and recovery scenarios is also recommended to validate that RSTP is functioning as intended where it is fully enabled and that compatibility modes are operating correctly where needed.

Properly managing backward compatibility during RSTP deployment ensures that the network can transition smoothly without unexpected outages or degraded performance. While RSTP brings significant improvements in speed and resilience, these benefits can only be fully realized when the network is consistently running the protocol end-to-end. Until that goal is reached, careful coordination between protocol versions, equipment capabilities, and configuration practices is necessary. Backward compatibility should not be viewed as a limitation, but rather as a bridge between the stability of legacy networks and the performance requirements of modern infrastructures. By respecting the design of older systems while planning for gradual evolution, network operators can build a seamless path toward a faster, more responsive Layer 2 environment.

Migrating from STP to RSTP

Migrating from the legacy Spanning Tree Protocol to Rapid Spanning Tree Protocol is a strategic step toward improving network convergence, enhancing fault tolerance, and reducing downtime in modern Ethernet infrastructures. As networks grow in complexity and applications demand higher availability and faster failover, the limitations of traditional STP become increasingly apparent. The migration process, while relatively straightforward in terms of protocol configuration, requires careful planning, a clear understanding of the operational differences, and a phased approach to avoid disruptions and ensure compatibility with existing hardware.

The first stage in migrating to RSTP involves a thorough assessment of the current network environment. This includes identifying all switches in the topology, documenting their hardware capabilities, and determining which devices support RSTP natively. Most enterprise-grade switches manufactured in the last decade support RSTP either by default or through a simple configuration change. However, older equipment may be limited to the 802.1D standard or may require a firmware upgrade to enable RSTP functionality. Compatibility checks are essential because any switch that does not support RSTP will force neighboring devices to revert to legacy STP behavior on the affected links, reducing the overall effectiveness of the protocol upgrade.

Once hardware capabilities are confirmed, the next step is to evaluate the network design and identify critical paths, redundant links, and areas that would benefit most from faster convergence. RSTP's strengths are best leveraged in environments where rapid failover is crucial, such as core-to-distribution links, access switches serving high-density user areas, and uplinks in data centers. Prioritizing these segments for early migration can yield immediate performance improvements while maintaining compatibility with the rest of the network. During this phase, administrators should also review current STP configurations, including bridge priorities, port costs, and timer settings, to ensure they align with best practices and are consistent across the environment.

Transitioning from STP to RSTP is typically accomplished by changing the spanning tree mode on each switch. On most platforms, this involves a command that sets the switch to use rapid-pvst, mst, or a similar variant depending on the desired spanning tree version and vendor implementation. This change should be made gradually and in a controlled manner. Ideally, the migration should begin at the core or distribution layers and proceed outward to the access layer. This top-down approach ensures that the root bridge and major path decisions are based on RSTP from the start, allowing the protocol to manage topology changes more efficiently as additional switches are brought into the new configuration.

During the migration, it is important to monitor the interaction between RSTP-enabled and STP-only switches. When an RSTP switch detects that its neighbor is running STP, it automatically falls back to 802.1D behavior on that specific port. This interoperability ensures stability, but it also means that rapid convergence features will not be active on those links. As a result, the full benefits of RSTP are only realized when the entire path between two points in the network is RSTP-capable. Therefore, documenting which links are still operating in legacy mode and gradually replacing or upgrading those switches should be part of the long-term migration plan.

Edge ports, known in STP as PortFast-enabled ports, also require attention during the migration. In RSTP, these ports should be explicitly configured as edge ports to allow immediate transition to the forwarding state. This is particularly important for access ports connected to end-user devices, VoIP phones, or wireless access points, where fast connectivity is essential. Failure to configure these ports correctly can result in unnecessary delays during device startup or reconnection. Administrators should audit existing PortFast configurations and ensure they are carried over to the RSTP environment using the proper edge port syntax supported by the switch vendor.

Security features such as BPDU Guard, Root Guard, and Loop Guard should be maintained and, where necessary, adapted to fit the new protocol. These features play a crucial role in protecting the network from misconfigurations and malicious activity during and after the migration. BPDU Guard, for instance, remains vital in preventing unauthorized switches from being connected to edge ports. Ensuring these features are enabled and tested as part of the migration helps preserve the integrity of the spanning tree and reduces the risk of loops and instability.

Testing is a critical component of the migration process. After enabling RSTP on a subset of switches, administrators should simulate topology changes such as link failures, switch reboots, and port disconnections to observe convergence behavior. Logs and debug outputs should be reviewed to confirm that ports transition through the expected RSTP states and that alternate paths are activated quickly when primary links fail. Metrics such as convergence time, link utilization, and BPDU traffic should be compared before and after the change to validate the performance gains.

Documentation should be updated continuously throughout the migration to reflect the current state of the network. This includes noting which switches are running RSTP, the status of each port, and any manual configurations made during the process. Accurate documentation is essential for troubleshooting, future upgrades, and ensuring that the network remains consistent and manageable over time.

After completing the migration, ongoing monitoring is necessary to ensure that the network continues to operate as expected. SNMP-based monitoring tools, syslog servers, and network management systems should be configured to alert administrators to topology changes, unexpected port role changes, and BPDU anomalies. Periodic reviews should be conducted to ensure that all devices are operating in

RSTP mode and that no ports remain stuck in compatibility mode due to legacy neighbors.

Migrating from STP to RSTP is not merely a technical upgrade but a strategic enhancement of the network's ability to respond to changes and deliver reliable service. When performed correctly, the migration results in a more agile, robust, and scalable Layer 2 topology that can support the demands of modern applications and evolving business needs. It enables rapid recovery from failures, reduces the administrative burden of manual tuning, and sets the stage for future innovations in network design and automation. With careful planning, thorough testing, and attention to detail, the transition to RSTP becomes a smooth and rewarding process that delivers measurable benefits to any network infrastructure.

Understanding MSTP Architecture

The Multiple Spanning Tree Protocol, or MSTP, represents a significant evolution in the spanning tree family of protocols by addressing the shortcomings of both traditional STP and its more modern counterpart, RSTP, when operating in complex VLAN-rich environments. MSTP, defined in the IEEE 802.1s standard and later integrated into the broader 802.1Q standard, was developed to provide scalability, flexibility, and more efficient use of network resources in large-scale Layer 2 topologies. At its core, MSTP introduces the concept of multiple spanning tree instances that can operate independently over the same physical topology, allowing different VLANs to follow different paths through the network, all while maintaining a loop-free architecture.

The traditional STP and RSTP models suffer from a fundamental inefficiency when used in networks with many VLANs. In those earlier protocols, each VLAN either shares a single spanning tree (in the case of STP and RSTP) or requires its own dedicated instance (as seen in Per-VLAN Spanning Tree Plus, or PVST+). While PVST+ allows load balancing across VLANs by letting each VLAN calculate its own spanning tree, it results in high CPU and memory utilization on switches due to the requirement to maintain a separate instance for every VLAN. MSTP resolves this by allowing VLANs to be grouped into a limited number of spanning tree instances called Multiple Spanning Tree Instances, or MSTIs. Each MSTI builds its own loop-free tree, and multiple VLANs can be mapped to a single instance, enabling a balance between efficient load sharing and resource conservation.

The architecture of MSTP is built around the concept of a region. An MST region is a group of interconnected switches that share the same configuration parameters, including the name of the region, the revision number, and the VLAN-to-instance mapping. All switches within the same region must have identical MST configurations; otherwise, they treat one another as if they were outside the region. This consistency ensures that the switches can correctly interpret and process the MST BPDUs that carry information about all spanning tree instances operating within the region. The configuration digest, which is a hash of the region parameters, allows each switch to verify that its neighbors are part of the same region. If two connected switches have a different digest, they cannot participate in the same MST region, and their link is treated as a legacy boundary.

Within an MST region, each instance calculates a separate spanning tree using the same basic algorithm as RSTP. MSTP inherits the fast convergence characteristics of RSTP, including the proposal and agreement handshake, rapid transition to forwarding, and the use of alternate and backup port roles. This means that MSTP combines the scalability of instance grouping with the speed and efficiency of rapid convergence, making it suitable for enterprise networks, metro Ethernet deployments, and large campus topologies. The region also maintains an Internal Spanning Tree, or IST, which serves as the foundational instance—typically instance 0—that all VLANs are associated with by default unless explicitly mapped to another instance.

The IST is crucial because it acts as the single spanning tree that connects the entire MST region to other regions or to legacy STP or RSTP domains. MSTP transmits BPDUs only for the IST outside the region, reducing protocol overhead and allowing the MST region to appear as a single bridge to neighboring non-MSTP switches. Internally, however, the region can manage multiple instances, each optimizing traffic paths for its assigned VLANs. This separation between internal complexity and external simplicity is one of MSTP's greatest strengths, enabling high performance and manageability without compromising interoperability.

A key component of understanding MSTP architecture is appreciating how VLANs are mapped to instances. Administrators must manually assign VLANs to MSTIs in a way that supports traffic engineering goals. For example, VLANs carrying voice traffic may be mapped to an instance that favors low-latency paths, while VLANs supporting backup services might be mapped to a different instance that prioritizes redundancy. This capability allows for intelligent load balancing across the network, as each instance can select different root bridges and designate different forwarding paths. Careful planning of the VLAN-to-instance mapping is essential, as all switches in the region must maintain the exact same mapping for the configuration to remain synchronized.

Another architectural consideration is the election of the root bridge per instance. Unlike traditional STP, where there is a single root bridge for the entire Layer 2 domain, MSTP allows each instance to have its own root. This enables greater control over how traffic flows for different services or departments within the organization. The root bridge election process follows the same rules as STP and RSTP, based on bridge priority and MAC address. By strategically configuring bridge priorities, administrators can ensure that different switches serve as the root for different instances, maximizing path utilization and minimizing congestion on any single segment of the network.

MSTP's region-aware architecture also simplifies interactions with legacy systems. Because MSTP emits only one set of BPDUs on boundary ports, it reduces the amount of protocol chatter between regions and helps maintain compatibility with older STP and RSTP domains. This allows organizations to migrate parts of the network to MSTP without disrupting the entire topology. Boundary ports automatically detect when they are connected to a non-MSTP switch and adjust their behavior accordingly, treating the external domain as a separate spanning tree and preventing loops across the region boundary.

Despite its complexity compared to earlier spanning tree protocols, MSTP is highly scalable. By limiting the number of instances—often to no more than 16—it avoids the processing overhead that comes with maintaining a spanning tree for every VLAN. The balance between flexibility and efficiency is one of the architectural hallmarks of MSTP. It allows network engineers to design robust, fault-tolerant topologies that scale with the growing demands of traffic segmentation, application-specific routing, and virtualized environments.

Understanding MSTP architecture is essential for any network professional working in enterprise or carrier-grade environments. It provides the tools necessary to build networks that are both agile and resilient, capable of supporting multiple traffic classes, balancing load across redundant links, and maintaining rapid convergence during topology changes. With MSTP, network designers gain a powerful protocol that respects the legacy foundations of spanning tree technology while providing the enhancements required to meet the challenges of modern Layer 2 networking.

Region Configuration and Mapping

In the context of Multiple Spanning Tree Protocol, the concept of a region plays a central role in how MSTP operates and scales across complex Layer 2 networks. MSTP regions are logical groupings of switches that share identical configuration parameters, which allow them to operate under a common MST domain. Understanding how to properly configure these regions and map VLANs to spanning tree instances within them is critical to achieving the flexibility, performance, and loop prevention goals that MSTP was designed to deliver. Proper region configuration and VLAN mapping provide the foundation for efficient traffic engineering, load balancing, and scalable network segmentation.

An MSTP region is defined by three key parameters: the region name, the configuration revision number, and the VLAN-to-instance mapping table. All switches within the same MSTP region must have exactly the same values for these three elements. If any one of these differs between two connected switches, they will treat each other as being in separate regions, and communication between them will default to the behavior used for boundary ports. This leads to increased complexity and may reduce the effectiveness of instance-based path optimization. For this reason, consistency in MST configuration across all devices in the same logical region is not just recommended—it is mandatory.

The region name is a simple text string that identifies the MST region. This name is locally configured and has no bearing on actual Layer 2 operations other than serving as a required element for configuration matching. The revision number is an integer value used as a versioning tool to track changes in configuration. While the revision number does not affect MSTP's forwarding behavior, it must match across all switches for them to be part of the same region. If the revision number differs, even by one digit, switches will compute a different configuration digest and consider each other to be outside the region. This can result in the creation of unnecessary spanning tree boundaries and may introduce suboptimal forwarding paths or increase convergence times.

The configuration digest is a cryptographic hash generated from the combination of the region name, revision number, and the VLAN-to-instance mapping. This digest is transmitted in MST BPDUs and allows each switch to verify that its neighbor is operating with a consistent configuration. If the digest received from a neighboring switch does not match the locally calculated digest, the switch assumes that it is connected to a different MST region and treats that link accordingly. Because the digest depends on all three parameters, any change in VLAN mappings, even if minor, requires the revision number to be incremented and updated across the entire region to ensure consistency and avoid unintended boundaries.

VLAN-to-instance mapping is where the real power of MSTP lies. Instead of assigning a unique spanning tree to every VLAN, administrators can group VLANs into a smaller number of instances called Multiple Spanning Tree Instances. Each MSTI operates independently and calculates its own loop-free topology. The goal is to segment traffic flows across different physical paths to make more efficient use of available bandwidth and to distribute the load among multiple root bridges. This is particularly useful in enterprise networks with multiple departments or services that require isolation but can benefit from distinct forwarding behaviors. For example, VLANs dedicated to voice traffic might be mapped to one instance that favors low-latency links, while VLANs for data backup could be mapped to another instance that prioritizes redundant, high-capacity paths.

The mapping process is entirely manual, which gives administrators full control but also requires careful planning. On each switch within the region, the VLANs must be explicitly assigned to one of the available instances. MSTP supports a limited number of instances—often up to 16—which makes it necessary to plan VLAN grouping thoughtfully. Assigning too many VLANs to a single instance might create a traffic bottleneck, while using too many instances can overburden the switch's CPU and memory. The best approach is to group VLANs based on similar traffic patterns, latency requirements, or logical business functions. Each switch must carry the same VLAN-to-instance mapping table to ensure a consistent view across the region and to avoid partitioning the region into mismatched segments.

Instance 0, also known as the Internal Spanning Tree, is the default instance to which all VLANs are assigned unless specified otherwise. The IST is used to communicate spanning tree information outside the region and represents the entire region as a single logical bridge to any legacy STP or RSTP domain. Because the IST carries the BPDUs seen outside the region, it must always remain stable and consistent. It also serves as the backbone for the region, providing foundational connectivity to all switches and enabling the inter-instance hierarchy that MSTP relies on. Even when other MSTIs are used for traffic engineering, the IST ensures overall topology cohesion and external interoperability.

In many cases, different MSTIs are configured to have different root bridges. This allows traffic for different VLANs to take different paths through the network, which would be impossible with standard STP or RSTP. By assigning lower bridge priorities for specific instances on different switches, administrators can control which switch becomes the root for each instance. This type of instance-level root bridge configuration is a powerful feature that must be supported by carefully planned region-wide configuration consistency. Without consistent mappings and properly designated root bridges, the benefits of MSTP's traffic distribution capabilities cannot be realized.

When MSTP regions are misconfigured, symptoms may include inconsistent BPDU behavior, ports stuck in blocking or inconsistent states, or VLANs appearing unreachable from certain parts of the network. These problems often trace back to mismatched region names, incorrect revision numbers, or misaligned VLAN-to-instance tables. Because the configuration digest prevents communication across mismatched configurations, even a minor error can lead to operational disruption. As such, network engineers must implement strict change control policies and use configuration templates or automation tools to ensure consistency across all MSTP-enabled switches.

Network monitoring and validation tools are essential during and after MSTP region deployment. These tools help verify that all switches share the same region parameters and that each VLAN is properly mapped. Commands that display the region name, revision number, and instance assignments should be used regularly to confirm the configuration. Troubleshooting is greatly simplified when documentation includes a detailed mapping of which VLANs are assigned to each instance and which switches are designated as root bridges for each MSTI.

Region configuration and VLAN-to-instance mapping are the heart of MSTP's flexibility and scalability. By defining logical boundaries, ensuring configuration uniformity, and optimizing traffic paths across multiple instances, MSTP enables the creation of agile Layer 2 networks that are both resilient and efficient. These regions function as autonomous spanning tree environments that can be tuned to meet the demands of complex, multi-service infrastructures. Mastery of region configuration and careful planning of VLAN mapping allows engineers to unlock the full potential of MSTP, providing intelligent traffic distribution, fault isolation, and seamless integration with legacy and modern network environments alike.

Instance-to-VLAN Assignment in MSTP

The ability to assign VLANs to multiple spanning tree instances is one of the most powerful and defining features of the Multiple Spanning Tree Protocol. This functionality enables network engineers to optimize Layer 2 topologies by customizing how traffic flows through the network based on service type, departmental segmentation, bandwidth needs, or performance requirements. Instead of forcing all VLANs to follow a single spanning tree, as in traditional STP or even RSTP, MSTP allows VLANs to be grouped into logical sets that each follow their own unique tree within a shared physical infrastructure. This provides the flexibility to balance load across redundant links and to make better use of available bandwidth while maintaining a loop-free environment.

The process of assigning VLANs to specific instances in MSTP begins with defining the Multiple Spanning Tree Instances themselves. Each instance is identified by a unique instance ID, typically a small integer starting from one. Every MSTP-enabled switch within a given MST region must share an identical mapping of VLANs to instance IDs. This uniformity is mandatory because MSTP relies on a consistent configuration digest to verify that switches belong to the same region. Any mismatch in the mapping table results in a failed digest comparison, which leads switches to treat one another as being outside the region. In that scenario, inter-switch links revert to legacy STP behavior, defeating the advantages MSTP was designed to provide.

The default state of all VLANs in MSTP is association with Instance 0, which is the Internal Spanning Tree. The IST is essential to the operation of MSTP because it serves as the control instance responsible for managing communication with external STP or RSTP devices and handling region-wide BPDUs. If no other mappings are specified, all VLANs will fall under the control of the IST and share its spanning tree, resulting in no traffic segmentation or load balancing. This might be suitable for small or static networks, but in larger or more dynamic environments, this approach limits the benefits of MSTP. The true value of MSTP lies in moving selected VLANs into other instances, where they can be controlled by different root bridges and follow different paths.

The assignment of VLANs to different instances should be done based on a thorough understanding of the traffic patterns and business logic within the network. For example, a company might assign VLANs used for voice traffic to Instance 1, VLANs used for high-speed data transfers to Instance 2, and VLANs for office applications to Instance 3. Each instance can then be optimized for latency, bandwidth, or fault tolerance depending on its use case. By assigning separate root bridges and adjusting path costs differently per instance, administrators can create a Layer 2 environment that supports real-time services, backup operations, and day-to-day business traffic without causing congestion or suboptimal routing.

One of the biggest operational advantages of instance-to-VLAN assignment is the ability to load balance across redundant links. In a network running a single spanning tree, redundant paths are blocked to prevent loops, which results in underutilized capacity. When VLANs are grouped into different instances, each instance can forward over a different physical path. As a result, all links can carry traffic simultaneously, provided that the traffic belongs to different VLANs assigned to different instances. This allows for much higher efficiency and better overall performance without compromising network integrity.

To implement VLAN-to-instance mapping, network engineers must configure the same mapping on all switches within the MST region. Most switches allow administrators to specify a range of VLANs and associate them with an instance ID using command-line or graphical interfaces. It is critical to ensure that every switch maintains the exact same mapping, including the range boundaries and instance numbers, otherwise they will calculate a different configuration digest and will not function as part of the same region. This strict requirement often necessitates the use of configuration templates or automation scripts to maintain uniformity across large networks.

In addition to assigning VLANs to instances, network engineers should also consider root bridge placement for each instance. By setting different bridge priorities for different instances on various switches, it is possible to influence which switch becomes the root bridge for a given instance. This strategy allows administrators to control the flow of traffic per VLAN group and to ensure that no single switch becomes a bottleneck. For instance, in a dual-core switch topology, one switch might be configured as the root for Instance 1 and the other as the root for Instance 2, thereby distributing the load and enhancing redundancy.

Monitoring and verifying instance-to-VLAN assignment is also a critical part of MSTP network operations. Most managed switches provide diagnostic commands that display the current mappings, the status of each instance, and the active topology. These outputs should be reviewed regularly to ensure that mappings are consistent and that traffic is being forwarded over the expected paths. If unexpected blocking or congestion occurs, it may be due to a misconfiguration in the VLAN mapping or root bridge assignment, both of which are easily rectified once the error is identified.

Instance-to-VLAN assignment is not only about performance—it also enhances fault isolation and service control. If an issue arises on one spanning tree instance, such as a topology change or link failure, the impact is limited to only those VLANs assigned to that instance. Other instances remain unaffected, which preserves service availability for unaffected departments or applications. This containment is particularly useful in service provider networks or large enterprise campuses where different customers or business units operate over shared infrastructure.

From a security standpoint, MSTP's ability to isolate and direct traffic based on instance assignments can also be leveraged to support network segmentation policies. VLANs belonging to sensitive departments, such as finance or human resources, can be grouped into a dedicated instance that is routed through controlled and monitored paths. This architecture minimizes exposure to lateral movement from compromised segments and supports compliance with internal security frameworks or industry regulations.

Ultimately, instance-to-VLAN assignment in MSTP provides network architects with a powerful tool to design Layer 2 environments that are both scalable and intelligent. By combining traffic engineering, root bridge control, and topological flexibility, MSTP allows networks to evolve beyond the limitations of traditional spanning tree designs. When applied correctly and managed consistently, VLAN-to-instance mapping enables a level of control and efficiency that is essential for modern networks handling diverse services and growing volumes of traffic. This strategic assignment is the key to unlocking the full potential of MSTP in any medium to large-scale Ethernet deployment.

Internal Spanning Tree in MSTP

The Internal Spanning Tree, commonly abbreviated as IST, is the foundational component of the Multiple Spanning Tree Protocol and plays a critical role in maintaining the stability, interoperability, and hierarchical control of the MSTP domain. Designated as instance 0 in every MST configuration, the IST is responsible for managing communication between the MST region and any external spanning tree domains. It acts as the unified representative of the entire region, ensuring that the region behaves as a single logical bridge to outside networks. While the MSTP architecture allows for the creation of multiple independent instances to support VLAN segmentation and traffic engineering, all of them rely on the IST for essential control plane coordination and topological coherence. Understanding the function, design, and impact of the IST is crucial for any engineer deploying or managing MSTP in production environments.

The Internal Spanning Tree serves as the primary bridge between internal MST operations and legacy spanning tree domains, including STP and RSTP. Because traditional STP does not understand the concept of multiple instances, the entire MST region must appear as a single switch to any legacy devices or non-MSTP regions. The IST fulfills this requirement by aggregating the status and topology of all MST instances and presenting them externally as a unified spanning tree. BPDUs originating from the IST are transmitted on all boundary ports, which are interfaces connecting the MST region to other domains. These BPDUs follow the traditional 802.1D format to ensure compatibility, and they contain a special MSTP-specific field that indicates the region's configuration digest and the revision number. This allows non-MSTP switches to interact with the MST region as though it were a standard STP switch while still allowing MSTP-enabled switches to exchange full instance information internally.

Internally, the IST is responsible for calculating and maintaining the core spanning tree that binds all switches within the MST region. It ensures that the region remains loop-free and converges quickly during topology changes. The IST uses the same mechanisms as RSTP, including port roles like root, designated, alternate, and backup, and it benefits from RSTP's rapid convergence techniques such as the proposal-agreement handshake. However, while other MST instances can forward traffic along their unique paths based on VLAN-to-instance assignments, they rely on the IST to maintain the overall connectivity of the region. If the IST becomes unstable or improperly configured, it can disrupt the communication not only between MSTP and external domains but also between internal instances that depend on its structure for synchronization and coordination.

In terms of root bridge election, the IST is considered the highest-level instance and often dictates the primary convergence behavior of the MST region. The root bridge for the IST is selected using the same criteria as other spanning tree variants, based on bridge priority and MAC address. This switch becomes the central point from which path costs are calculated for the IST, and all other switches determine their best path to the root using cumulative link costs. Because the IST impacts how external devices perceive the MST region, selecting the appropriate switch to act as the IST root is a critical design decision. It is often recommended that a central, highly available, and well-connected core switch be designated as the root for the IST to ensure efficient path selection and minimize failover times.

The structure of the IST also affects the behavior of other MST instances. While each MSTI calculates its own independent tree, it is constrained by the IST's topology in certain scenarios. For example, if a link is blocked in the IST due to its cost or to prevent a loop, that link cannot be used by any other MSTI, even if it would be the preferred path for VLANs assigned to that instance. This interdependence means that while MSTP offers significant flexibility through multiple instances, the IST still serves as the controlling layer and can impose limitations on alternate trees. As such, network engineers must carefully design the IST to complement the needs of higher-numbered instances rather than inadvertently constrain them.

Another important consideration in the operation of the IST is the transmission and processing of BPDUs. The IST is the only instance that generates BPDUs visible to external switches. These BPDUs carry the configuration digest, revision level, and essential instance synchronization information, allowing other MSTP switches to verify that their neighbor belongs to the same region. If a switch receives an IST BPDU with a mismatched digest, it considers the neighbor to be part of a different region and establishes a boundary on that port. This boundary formation prevents instance information from crossing into mismatched regions and ensures that loops are avoided. This behavior makes the IST a critical factor not only for spanning tree calculations but also for enforcing the logical separation between MST regions.

All VLANs that are not explicitly assigned to another instance are automatically included in the IST. This default behavior ensures that no VLAN is left unprotected by a spanning tree and that even simple configurations benefit from loop prevention. However, relying too heavily on the IST for all VLANs can negate the performance and load balancing benefits that MSTP is designed to provide. Best practices dictate that traffic-intensive or latency-sensitive VLANs be moved to their own instances where custom topologies can be implemented. Even then, those instances will continue to rely on the IST for inter-switch coordination and for external path resolution.

During network changes such as switch additions, firmware upgrades, or topology modifications, the stability of the IST must be preserved. Changes to the IST root bridge, incorrect cost assignments, or link flaps can lead to region-wide instability. Because the IST is the control plane anchor for all other instances, any disruption in its operation can cascade into multiple MSTIs, resulting in widespread traffic loss or delays. For this reason, ongoing monitoring of the IST's status, BPDU consistency, and root bridge placement is essential for maintaining a healthy MSTP deployment. Network management tools should be used to track IST path costs, detect role transitions, and confirm that all devices are operating with a synchronized configuration digest.

The Internal Spanning Tree is not just another instance in MSTP; it is the backbone of the entire protocol structure. It manages external communication, ensures regional cohesion, and provides the logical framework within which all other instances operate. Its unique responsibilities make it the most critical instance in any MST configuration. A well-designed IST enhances the performance, stability, and scalability of the MST region, while a poorly designed or misconfigured IST can severely hinder network efficiency and reliability. For network architects and administrators, a deep understanding of the IST's function, interaction with other instances, and influence on overall network behavior is essential to building a successful and resilient Layer 2 architecture using Multiple Spanning Tree Protocol.

Interoperability Between STP, RSTP, and MSTP

In real-world networks, it is common to encounter environments where different spanning tree protocol versions must coexist. Whether due to phased upgrades, multi-vendor deployments, or legacy hardware, network administrators are often tasked with ensuring seamless interoperability between Standard Spanning Tree Protocol (STP, IEEE 802.1D), Rapid Spanning Tree Protocol (RSTP, IEEE 802.1w), and Multiple Spanning Tree Protocol (MSTP, IEEE 802.1s). Achieving stable and functional interoperability among these protocols requires a detailed understanding of how each operates, how they interact across boundaries, and what considerations must be taken into account to avoid misconfigurations, loops, or degraded convergence times. Each protocol interprets and forwards Bridge Protocol Data Units differently, and the challenge lies in harmonizing their behavior without breaking the fundamental loop prevention mechanism that the spanning tree family guarantees.

STP, the original spanning tree standard, operates using a timer-based model where ports transition through multiple states before becoming forwarding. It sends configuration BPDUs every two seconds from the root bridge and requires ports to wait for specific timer expirations before transitioning to forwarding after a topology change. This model is deterministic but slow, often requiring up to 50 seconds to reconverge. STP also sends BPDUs only from the root bridge, and downstream switches do not originate BPDUs unless they believe they are the root, which limits STP's ability to detect certain failures quickly.

RSTP improves upon STP by introducing faster convergence mechanisms and modifying the BPDU behavior. In RSTP, BPDUs are sent by all switches, not just the root, and ports can negotiate rapid transitions to forwarding through a handshake using proposal and agreement messages. It introduces new port roles such as alternate and backup and eliminates the listening state, combining it with blocking into a single discarding state. Despite these changes, RSTP remains compatible with STP through a carefully designed fallback mechanism. When an RSTP switch detects that its neighbor is operating with standard STP, it reverts to STP behavior on that port. This allows RSTP switches to interoperate with STP switches while preserving protocol integrity and preventing topology loops. However, in such hybrid links, rapid convergence features are not used, and the port behaves as if it were part of an STP domain.

MSTP builds upon the RSTP framework and introduces the concept of regions and multiple instances. Internally, MSTP uses RSTP mechanisms for fast convergence and port roles. Externally, MSTP must maintain compatibility with both STP and RSTP by exposing its Internal Spanning Tree (IST) as a single logical bridge. This ensures that MSTP appears as a traditional spanning tree switch to any legacy neighbor. MSTP achieves this by sending only one set of BPDUs on boundary ports, formatted in a way that is understandable to both STP and RSTP devices. These BPDUs include the region's configuration digest and revision number, which are ignored by legacy devices but used by MSTP-capable neighbors to verify region membership.

Interoperability between MSTP and STP or RSTP occurs at the boundary of the MST region. A boundary port is any interface connecting an MSTP switch to a non-MSTP switch. The MSTP switch must detect that the neighbor is using a different protocol version and modify its behavior accordingly. On such ports, the MSTP switch sends only IST BPDUs and disables the transmission of instance-specific information. These ports are excluded from all MSTIs except the IST, and only the control plane of instance 0 participates in the spanning tree. This allows MSTP regions to present themselves as a single bridge entity to the outside world while internally maintaining multiple logical topologies.

In a mixed environment, one of the most critical considerations is the consistent placement of the root bridge. Since STP, RSTP, and MSTP all elect a root bridge based on bridge ID and priority, it is essential that the intended root has the lowest priority across all domains. If the root bridge is unintentionally located inside an STP domain or outside the intended MSTP region, traffic flow can become inefficient, and topology stability may be compromised. For instance, if an MSTP region connects to an STP switch that mistakenly becomes the root, all VLAN traffic from the MSTP region will flow toward the STP switch's location, potentially congesting links and undermining redundancy. Therefore, administrators should manually configure bridge priorities and monitor root bridge status to ensure that the correct switch assumes this role.

Path cost discrepancies can also affect interoperability. STP and RSTP use the same cost metrics, but some vendors allow the use of revised path cost formulas to support higher-speed links like 10 Gbps or 100 Gbps. MSTP, while internally consistent, must align its cost calculations on boundary ports with those expected by the neighboring STP or RSTP device. Failure to do so may cause one side to block a port while the other forwards, resulting in unidirectional connectivity or suboptimal paths. Manual tuning of port cost values is sometimes required to ensure that both devices agree on the same path selection.

Port configuration features like PortFast, BPDU Guard, and Root Guard must also be carefully evaluated in mixed-protocol environments. For example, PortFast or edge port behavior in MSTP must not be enabled on links connecting to legacy STP switches, as these links must participate in topology negotiation. Similarly, enabling BPDU Guard on a boundary port can result in the port being shut down if it receives legitimate BPDUs from a neighboring STP switch. Root Guard, on the other hand, can be a useful tool to prevent external devices from claiming the root bridge role, which is especially important when MSTP regions connect to unmanaged or third-party equipment.

Troubleshooting interoperability issues requires visibility into each protocol's behavior. MSTP switches often include diagnostic tools to show whether a port is in MSTP, RSTP, or STP mode, based on the type of BPDU received. Logs and status commands help administrators verify that the expected protocol fallback has occurred and that the link is stable. Network monitoring tools should be configured to alert on topology changes, unexpected root role transitions, or high BPDU activity, which may indicate misconfigurations or compatibility problems.

The key to successful interoperability between STP, RSTP, and MSTP lies in deliberate design, consistent configuration, and ongoing monitoring. Mixed-protocol environments must be treated as transitional stages, with clear documentation and plans for eventual standardization. Whether migrating from STP to RSTP or integrating MSTP into an older infrastructure, the goal is to maintain network stability while gradually adopting modern, more efficient protocols. By understanding the operational nuances of each protocol and their behavior at interoperability boundaries, network engineers can ensure that these technologies work together seamlessly, delivering reliable and scalable Layer 2 connectivity across diverse and evolving network topologies.

Scalability Benefits of MSTP

The Multiple Spanning Tree Protocol was designed to address the inherent limitations of traditional spanning tree implementations in large-scale Layer 2 networks. As networks expanded and VLAN segmentation became increasingly common, the need for a more scalable solution became evident. MSTP emerged as the protocol of choice for enterprise and service provider environments that require logical traffic separation, efficient use of physical links, and consistent loop prevention across large and dynamic topologies. Its architectural design introduces several mechanisms that enable it to scale more effectively than its predecessors, including the use of multiple spanning tree instances, optimized BPDU handling, and the concept of regions. These features combine to provide a scalable framework that can support hundreds of VLANs without overwhelming switch resources or compromising performance.

One of the most impactful scalability features of MSTP is its use of Multiple Spanning Tree Instances, which decouples the control plane of the spanning tree from the sheer number of VLANs present in a network. In older protocols such as Per-VLAN Spanning Tree Plus, a separate spanning tree instance had to be maintained for each VLAN. This design placed significant burdens on the CPU and memory of network devices, as every instance required independent computation, state tracking, and BPDU transmission. MSTP resolves this inefficiency by allowing administrators to map multiple VLANs to a single spanning tree instance. As a result, only a limited and manageable number of spanning tree instances need to be maintained, even in networks with hundreds or thousands of VLANs. This consolidation dramatically reduces the resource consumption of each switch, freeing up processing power and memory for other critical tasks and allowing the network to grow without linear increases in complexity.

The scalability advantages of MSTP are also evident in its efficient use of BPDUs. In traditional STP and RSTP, BPDUs are transmitted on a per-VLAN basis. In large environments, this leads to a flood of control plane traffic, as every switch sends a separate BPDU for every VLAN on every trunk link. MSTP reduces this overhead by sending a single BPDU per region, regardless of how many VLANs are present. This BPDU includes information for all active spanning tree instances, encapsulated in a compact format that ensures both efficiency and clarity. By aggregating BPDU communication in this way, MSTP reduces bandwidth consumption on management interfaces and lowers the risk of BPDU loss or misinterpretation, especially during network instability or convergence events. Fewer BPDUs also mean reduced load on the control plane and fewer chances for protocol-related errors to affect the forwarding logic.

Another scalability feature of MSTP lies in its region-based architecture. MSTP divides the network into logical regions, with each region acting as a single virtual bridge when interacting with external STP or RSTP domains. This allows for hierarchical control and simplifies inter-domain spanning tree communication. From the outside, the entire MST region appears as one logical switch, with only the Internal Spanning Tree responsible for participating in external topology calculations. Internally, however, the region can contain multiple switches, each participating in several instances based on their VLAN assignments. This abstraction allows MSTP to scale across wide and complex networks without overwhelming neighboring spanning tree domains. It also enables modular network designs, where each region can be tuned for local optimization while preserving end-to-end stability.

MSTP's scalability is further enhanced by its ability to enable load balancing and traffic engineering across redundant links. In legacy spanning tree designs, redundant links are often blocked to prevent loops, resulting in idle bandwidth and wasted infrastructure. MSTP allows different spanning tree instances to use different root bridges and different forwarding paths, enabling the network to utilize multiple physical links simultaneously. This not only improves performance and throughput but also distributes the processing and forwarding load across the network. When designed correctly, each instance can be associated with specific VLANs that follow distinct paths, reducing congestion and improving the scalability of traffic delivery in high-demand environments.

The protocol also introduces enhancements in convergence and fault recovery that support scalability indirectly. By using Rapid Spanning Tree mechanics within each instance, MSTP enables fast failover and minimizes service disruption. Fast convergence is particularly important in large-scale environments, where traditional timer-based STP would take too long to recover, potentially impacting hundreds of VLANs and thousands of endpoints. With MSTP, only the affected instance undergoes recalculation, rather than triggering a global reconvergence. This isolation of failure domains reduces the risk of cascading failures and allows the network to scale without magnifying the impact of individual faults.

MSTP also offers scalability in configuration and management. Rather than managing individual VLANs on a one-to-one basis with spanning tree settings, network administrators can group VLANs based on common traffic patterns or service types and assign them to a single instance. This logical grouping reduces the number of configurations that must be maintained and audited. In environments with automation or template-based configuration tools, MSTP enables efficient management at scale, as bulk VLAN assignments and instance properties can be defined once and propagated across the entire region. This reduces human error and simplifies operations, allowing engineers to manage more VLANs and switches with less effort and risk.

Even in environments that require interoperability with legacy devices, MSTP maintains its scalability benefits. By isolating protocol interaction to the Internal Spanning Tree and presenting a unified bridge to STP or RSTP devices, MSTP minimizes the complexity of mixed environments. This allows for gradual upgrades and supports the coexistence of modern and older infrastructure without compromising the overall scalability of the design. MSTP boundary ports serve as controlled gateways, where region-specific logic is translated into a form compatible with external domains. This structure ensures that the scalable benefits of MSTP are preserved internally, while maintaining stability and compatibility externally.

As network demands continue to increase due to the growth of cloud services, data-intensive applications, and virtualization, the scalability of the control plane becomes as critical as that of the data plane. MSTP provides a scalable solution that aligns with these requirements, offering both the architectural flexibility and operational efficiency needed to manage large and segmented Layer 2 networks. By optimizing how VLANs are grouped, how control traffic is transmitted, and how topology is calculated, MSTP enables networks to scale in both size and performance without sacrificing manageability or reliability. This makes it a vital protocol for modern enterprises and service providers building the next generation of agile and resilient Ethernet infrastructures.

Best Practices for MSTP Deployment

Deploying Multiple Spanning Tree Protocol effectively requires a strategic approach that balances performance, redundancy, scalability, and manageability. MSTP introduces complexity beyond traditional STP and RSTP because of its use of instances, regions, and VLAN-to-instance mappings, but when configured correctly, it provides a highly flexible and scalable solution for modern Layer 2 networks. Adhering to well-established best practices ensures that MSTP is not only stable and secure but also optimized to take full advantage of its capabilities without causing unintended loops, convergence delays, or misconfigurations.

The foundation of any MSTP deployment begins with defining a consistent and well-documented region configuration. All switches that participate in the same MST region must have identical configurations for the region name, revision number, and VLAN-to-instance mapping. This uniformity is critical because MSTP uses a configuration digest—a hash of these three elements—to validate that switches belong to the same region. A mismatch in any of these parameters will cause MSTP to treat a neighbor switch as part of a different region, which results in boundary formation and limits the benefits of MSTP's instance-based flexibility. For this reason, administrators should use templates or centralized management tools to ensure configuration consistency across the entire region and establish strict controls around change management to prevent accidental misalignments.

Mapping VLANs to spanning tree instances must also be approached with careful planning. While the default behavior places all VLANs into the Internal Spanning Tree, this configuration misses the opportunity to use MSTP's true potential. VLANs should be logically grouped based on their traffic patterns, service types, or organizational roles, and then assigned to different MST instances. For example, production traffic, voice traffic, and backup traffic can each be placed into separate instances, with their own root bridges and preferred paths. This design allows multiple links in the network to be actively used, distributing traffic loads and increasing fault tolerance. However, care must be taken not to overload a single instance with too many VLANs, which could concentrate traffic and negate the performance gains from traffic separation.

Root bridge placement for each instance is another critical design decision that directly influences traffic flow and network efficiency. MSTP allows each instance to have its own root bridge, which determines the direction of forwarding paths for VLANs assigned to that instance. By strategically placing the root bridges for different instances on different core switches, traffic can be balanced across multiple uplinks, and redundant paths can be utilized more effectively. To enforce root bridge selection, the bridge priority value should be explicitly configured for each instance, rather than relying on default values that might lead to unpredictable results. Backup root bridge placement should also be considered, ensuring that if the primary root bridge fails, the topology can quickly reconverge using a switch that maintains logical traffic paths.

Proper configuration of edge ports and boundary ports is essential to prevent unnecessary topology recalculations and to secure the network against misbehaving devices. Ports connected to end-user devices, such as workstations, printers, or IP phones, should be explicitly configured as edge ports. This designation allows them to transition immediately to the forwarding state upon link-up, improving convergence speed and reducing the chance of loops. To protect edge ports from inadvertently introducing loops if another switch is connected, BPDU Guard should be enabled. This feature disables the port immediately upon detecting a BPDU, which helps prevent user error or malicious attempts to tamper with the network topology.

Boundary ports, which connect the MST region to devices running legacy STP or RSTP, should be properly recognized and managed. These ports only participate in instance 0, the Internal Spanning Tree, and must maintain a consistent and stable connection to external domains. Enabling Root Guard on these ports can help prevent a switch outside the MST region from becoming the root bridge, which would disrupt instance-level traffic engineering. Additionally, administrators should validate that all boundary ports are correctly classified and monitored, as instability on these links can affect not only instance 0 but also the overall performance of the MST region.

Consistent path cost settings across the network are necessary to maintain predictable topology calculations. While MSTP uses the same cost metrics as RSTP, variations in link speed or manual overrides can lead to asymmetric paths and unintended blocking behavior. It is a best practice to standardize path costs across similar link types and to explicitly configure port costs where precise traffic engineering is required. For example, if a certain link should be preferred for voice traffic in a given instance, its cost should be set lower for that instance than for other available paths. Careful cost tuning allows MSTP to direct traffic in a controlled manner, minimizing congestion and improving the overall efficiency of the network.

Documentation and monitoring are also critical components of a successful MSTP deployment. Every change to instance mappings, root bridge placement, and cost configurations should be recorded and reflected in network diagrams. Monitoring tools should be configured to track topology changes, port roles, root bridge status, and BPDU activity. Alerts can help identify instability, configuration mismatches, or unauthorized devices attempting to influence the topology. Regular audits and simulations of failure scenarios should be conducted to validate that the spanning tree behaves as expected and that redundancy plans are functioning correctly.

Lastly, training and operational readiness are vital for maintaining a stable MSTP deployment over time. Network engineers and administrators should be familiar with MSTP concepts and commands on the specific hardware platforms in use. Understanding how to interpret port roles, instance status, and spanning tree metrics helps teams diagnose problems quickly and apply changes with confidence. In organizations that support automation and scripting, integrating MSTP configuration into infrastructure-as-code workflows can further reduce errors and accelerate deployment.

Deploying MSTP is a sophisticated process that brings significant rewards when done correctly. By adhering to best practices that focus on consistency, logical design, protection mechanisms, and active monitoring, organizations can build Layer 2 networks that are both resilient and efficient. MSTP enables advanced control of traffic flow, improves utilization of physical infrastructure, and offers faster recovery from topology changes, making it an ideal solution for complex enterprise networks with high availability requirements.

Designing Redundant Layer 2 Networks

Redundancy in Layer 2 networks is fundamental to ensuring high availability, minimizing downtime, and maintaining business continuity in enterprise and service provider environments. A well-designed redundant Layer 2 network can withstand link failures, device outages, and unexpected disruptions without significantly affecting end-user connectivity or service quality. However, achieving effective redundancy at this layer requires more than simply adding extra links or backup switches. It demands a strategic architectural approach, a deep understanding of protocol behavior, and precise configuration of network elements to ensure that traffic flows efficiently and loops are prevented. The key to success lies in balancing redundancy with control, ensuring that the benefits of fault tolerance do not introduce complexity or instability.

At the heart of redundant Layer 2 design is the need to avoid loops. Ethernet, by design, lacks a native mechanism for detecting and dropping looping frames. A frame caught in a loop can circulate indefinitely, leading to broadcast storms that overwhelm switches, consume bandwidth, and bring down the network. To solve this, spanning tree protocols are used to selectively block redundant paths and maintain a loop-free topology. However, this comes at the cost of underutilizing available links, since some connections remain idle during normal operation. Designing a redundant Layer 2 topology, therefore, involves not only building physical redundancy but also ensuring that logical paths are optimized and that the protocol used for loop prevention can recover quickly from topology changes.

Spanning Tree Protocol, and its more modern variants such as Rapid Spanning Tree Protocol and Multiple Spanning Tree Protocol, are central to redundancy in Layer 2. RSTP offers fast convergence and is ideal for environments that require rapid failover. MSTP, on the other hand, enables load balancing by allowing different VLANs to use different spanning tree instances. When designing redundancy into the network, it is essential to select the appropriate protocol for the size and complexity of the environment. For smaller, flat networks, RSTP may suffice. In larger, segmented networks with many VLANs and distribution layers, MSTP offers greater flexibility and scalability.

A well-structured redundant Layer 2 design follows a hierarchical model. The most common model includes core, distribution, and access layers. Redundancy is built in horizontally and vertically within this structure. At the access layer, each switch should be dual-homed to two distribution switches. This ensures that if one distribution switch fails, the access switch can still reach the core. Distribution switches, in turn, should be redundantly connected to the core. This dual-homing not only provides physical redundancy but also allows spanning tree to calculate alternate paths that can be activated in the event of a failure.

Root bridge placement is a crucial decision in any redundant design. The root bridge is the logical center of the spanning tree, and all path costs are calculated relative to it. In a dual-core design, it is common to configure one core switch as the primary root bridge and the other as the secondary. This ensures a predictable and optimized topology, with traffic flowing through designated links. In MSTP, each instance can have a different root bridge, allowing traffic for different VLANs to take different paths, further enhancing redundancy and load distribution. Manual configuration of bridge priority values is necessary to enforce root bridge roles and to avoid unwanted root bridge elections that can destabilize the network.

Link aggregation is another method used to build redundancy at Layer 2. Technologies such as EtherChannel or Link Aggregation Control Protocol allow multiple physical links to be bundled into a single logical interface. This provides both redundancy and increased bandwidth. If one link in the bundle fails, traffic continues to flow across the remaining links without triggering a spanning tree recalculation. Link aggregation is especially useful on trunk links between distribution and core switches, where high availability and performance are critical.

Designing for fast convergence is essential in redundant Layer 2 networks. Even with physical redundancy in place, slow protocol responses can lead to service interruptions. Rapid transitions to forwarding state, fast detection of link failures, and minimal topology disruption are all necessary for achieving high availability. In RSTP and MSTP, edge ports should be clearly defined, and features such as PortFast, UplinkFast, and Loop Guard should be used to accelerate convergence and protect the network from unexpected behavior. Edge ports transition immediately to the forwarding state, reducing downtime for end-user devices. Loop Guard prevents ports from erroneously transitioning to forwarding due to missed BPDUs, which can occur during unidirectional link failures.

Careful path cost tuning helps shape the logical topology and ensures that redundant paths are used appropriately. Administrators can adjust path cost values to influence which links are preferred for forwarding and which are placed into a blocking state. This tuning allows for load sharing and can direct traffic across preferred routes based on application needs or link capacities. Path costs must be consistent and predictable to prevent suboptimal path selection or asymmetric routing.

Redundant Layer 2 designs must also account for failure domains and their containment. The goal is to localize the impact of a failure so that it does not propagate across the entire network. This is achieved by segmenting the network using VLANs, employing multiple MST instances, and designing distribution layers to isolate access layer faults. In this way, a failure in one part of the network affects only a limited number of devices or services, and the rest of the infrastructure continues to function normally. This containment is especially important in environments such as campuses, data centers, and industrial networks, where uptime and service continuity are paramount.

Visibility and monitoring are vital components of maintaining a redundant Layer 2 network. Administrators must be able to detect failures quickly, identify which paths are active, and verify that spanning tree roles and states are correct. Tools that provide real-time topology views, BPDU statistics, and port role information are invaluable for diagnosing issues and ensuring that redundancy mechanisms are working as intended. Logging of topology changes and alerts for state transitions help identify problematic links or devices before they cause widespread outages.

Redundancy should also be planned with future growth in mind. Networks evolve, and a design that works today may not scale effectively tomorrow. Modular design, standardization of configurations, and documentation of root bridge placement and instance mappings make it easier to expand the network without compromising redundancy. New switches can be added to the access layer, new VLANs can be assigned to existing instances, and new redundant links can be brought online with minimal disruption, provided the foundational design is solid.

A redundant Layer 2 network is more than just an insurance policy against hardware failure. It is a proactive design strategy that ensures service continuity, supports dynamic traffic patterns, and enables organizations to grow and adapt without rearchitecting their entire infrastructure. By combining sound physical design with logical control through spanning tree protocols, administrators can build networks that are both resilient and efficient, capable of supporting modern applications and critical services in a constantly evolving technological landscape.

Understanding TRILL Architecture

The Transparent Interconnection of Lots of Links, commonly known as TRILL, represents a fundamental rethinking of how Layer 2 networks can be built and operated in modern data centers and large-scale environments. TRILL was developed by the Internet Engineering Task Force to address the limitations of traditional spanning tree-based Ethernet networks, particularly in scenarios that require scalability, efficient link utilization, and fast convergence. The architecture of TRILL blends the simplicity of Ethernet with the power and flexibility of link-state routing protocols, creating a hybrid model that eliminates many of the drawbacks historically associated with loop prevention mechanisms like STP, RSTP, or MSTP.

At the heart of TRILL's architecture is the concept of replacing the spanning tree approach with a routing-based method to forward Layer 2 frames. Rather than relying on a single active path and blocking redundant ones to prevent loops, TRILL allows all available paths to be active and used for forwarding traffic. This is achieved by encapsulating Ethernet frames with a TRILL header and routing them through a fabric of devices known as RBridges or Routing Bridges. These RBridges form a control plane using the IS-IS link-state routing protocol, which allows each RBridge to have a complete view of the network topology and make intelligent forwarding decisions based on the shortest path to the destination.

TRILL's use of IS-IS is one of its defining architectural choices. IS-IS was selected due to its suitability for link-state operations in environments with variable topologies and its ability to operate independently of IP addressing. Each RBridge in the network advertises its connectivity through IS-IS link-state advertisements, which include information about its neighbors and reachable destinations. This information is used to construct a complete topology map across all participating RBridges. As a result, every RBridge knows the best path to every other RBridge, and this path calculation is performed using the well-known Dijkstra algorithm, which identifies the shortest and most efficient routes through the network.

To carry Ethernet frames through the TRILL network, a method of encapsulation is required. When a frame enters the TRILL domain at an ingress RBridge, the RBridge adds a TRILL header that includes the ID of the egress RBridge, as well as a hop count and other control information. This encapsulated frame is then forwarded through the network based on the shortest path to the destination RBridge, rather than relying on traditional MAC address learning and flooding mechanisms. Once the frame reaches the egress RBridge, the TRILL header is removed and the original Ethernet frame is delivered to its final destination. This approach effectively turns the Layer 2 network into a routed fabric, eliminating many of the inefficiencies and scaling limitations of conventional Ethernet switching.

One of the most significant advantages of TRILL architecture is its ability to perform multipathing at Layer 2. Because all links are active and the control plane is based on a full topology view, TRILL can perform equal-cost multipath routing, allowing multiple paths to be used concurrently between any two RBridges. This greatly enhances bandwidth utilization, improves fault tolerance, and supports higher throughput across the fabric. Traditional spanning tree networks cannot do this, as they rely on blocking redundant paths to prevent loops, leaving much of the physical infrastructure idle during normal operation.

Loop prevention in TRILL is achieved through its routing logic and hop count mechanism. Unlike spanning tree protocols, which detect loops by disabling links and waiting for timer-based recalculations, TRILL inherently prevents loops by ensuring that each frame has a limited number of hops it can traverse. Each RBridge decrements the hop count as the frame is forwarded, and if the hop count reaches zero before reaching the destination, the frame is discarded. Additionally, since the forwarding decisions are based on the calculated paths from the link-state database, frames cannot endlessly loop because they are always guided by a deterministic and loop-free route calculation.

TRILL also improves convergence times in the event of a topology change. Because IS-IS maintains a synchronized view of the network across all RBridges, changes in link status are quickly propagated and recalculated across the entire topology. This allows the network to respond dynamically and rapidly to link or node failures without the need for blocked paths to be re-enabled or for ports to transition through spanning tree states. The result is a network that can recover from disruptions in milliseconds, rather than the seconds or tens of seconds often associated with spanning tree-based topologies.

Another important aspect of TRILL architecture is its support for MAC address learning. Although TRILL functions as a routing protocol, it still supports traditional Ethernet frame delivery semantics. When a frame with an unknown destination MAC address enters the network, the ingress RBridge can flood it within the TRILL domain using controlled multicast forwarding. Once the destination responds, MAC learning occurs, and future frames are forwarded directly through the shortest path. This hybrid model allows TRILL to maintain compatibility with legacy Ethernet devices while still taking advantage of advanced routing features within the TRILL domain.

The architecture of TRILL is also designed with scalability in mind. By decoupling the data plane from the MAC address table size and by allowing multiple paths for traffic, TRILL can support larger networks with more devices, more VLANs, and more traffic flows. Traditional Ethernet switching becomes cumbersome at scale due to the limited capacity of MAC tables, the inefficiency of broadcast and unknown unicast flooding, and the slow convergence of spanning tree recalculations. TRILL solves these problems by routing frames intelligently and by limiting the use of flooding to only those cases where it is strictly necessary.

Furthermore, TRILL supports integration with higher-layer network virtualization and tunneling technologies. It can serve as a foundation for data center fabrics, especially in scenarios where east-west traffic between servers must be delivered quickly and predictably. With its built-in support for VLAN tagging, loop prevention, multipathing, and fast convergence, TRILL is well suited to modern data center needs, offering a scalable and efficient solution that aligns with the performance and reliability requirements of virtualized environments, storage networks, and high-performance computing clusters.

TRILL's architecture represents a convergence of the benefits of Ethernet and IP routing. It preserves the plug-and-play simplicity of Ethernet at the edges while introducing the robust control plane and path optimization features of routing in the core. This duality allows network designers to build Layer 2 domains that behave more like Layer 3 networks in terms of stability, scale, and efficiency. As data centers continue to evolve toward distributed, cloud-native architectures, understanding the inner workings of TRILL provides a foundation for adopting more intelligent and agile network designs that go beyond the limitations of spanning tree-based approaches.

TRILL as an Evolution of Spanning Tree

The evolution of Layer 2 networking has been driven by the growing demands of scalability, availability, and performance in enterprise and data center environments. For many years, the Spanning Tree Protocol and its variants such as Rapid Spanning Tree Protocol and Multiple Spanning Tree Protocol served as the cornerstone of loop prevention and topology management in Ethernet networks. These protocols established a foundational mechanism to ensure a loop-free topology by selectively blocking redundant paths and maintaining a single active path between any two points. While this approach offered stability and reliability, it inherently underutilized the available bandwidth, limited scalability, and responded slowly to topology changes. As data centers began to host more virtual machines, support high-throughput applications, and require fast convergence, the limitations of spanning tree-based designs became more pronounced. It was in response to these growing needs that TRILL, or Transparent Interconnection of Lots of Links, emerged as a natural evolution of spanning tree, introducing a revolutionary approach that blends the simplicity of Ethernet with the intelligence of routing.

TRILL redefines how Layer 2 networks operate by eliminating the need for spanning tree-based loop prevention. Instead of blocking redundant paths, TRILL uses a routing-based model that enables all links to be active and available for traffic forwarding. This represents a significant departure from the traditional behavior of spanning tree protocols. In spanning tree networks, link redundancy exists for failover purposes but not for active use, leading to wasted bandwidth and unequal load distribution. TRILL overcomes this by enabling multipath forwarding through the use of a link-state routing protocol, specifically IS-IS, which provides each TRILL device, known as a Routing Bridge or RBridge, with a comprehensive view of the network topology.

The use of IS-IS in TRILL provides the intelligence necessary to calculate shortest path forwarding through a routed control plane. Each RBridge participates in the IS-IS control plane and exchanges link-state advertisements with its peers, resulting in a synchronized topology database across the entire TRILL domain. This distributed knowledge enables each RBridge to compute the optimal path to any other RBridge in the network using the Dijkstra algorithm. Frames are no longer forwarded based on learned MAC address paths from a flat table but are instead encapsulated and routed through the network based on these calculated shortest paths. This routing behavior is fundamentally more scalable and efficient than the reactive and timer-driven mechanisms of spanning tree.

Another transformative improvement TRILL brings over spanning tree is its use of encapsulation to separate the transit behavior of frames from their original Ethernet format. When a frame enters a TRILL network at an ingress RBridge, it is encapsulated with a TRILL header that includes the address of the egress RBridge, along with control information such as hop count and path indicators. This encapsulation allows the frame to traverse the TRILL fabric as a routed packet, unaffected by traditional Layer 2 limitations like broadcast domains or MAC address learning on intermediate devices. Upon reaching the egress RBridge, the TRILL header is removed, and the original Ethernet frame is delivered to the destination as usual. This architectural design effectively transforms the Layer 2 domain into a logical routed network while preserving compatibility with existing Ethernet-based systems.

One of the most critical aspects where TRILL surpasses spanning tree is in its support for equal-cost multipath (ECMP). Traditional spanning tree protocols can only maintain a single active path between any two switches, placing all other redundant paths into a blocking state to avoid loops. This results in a topology where multiple physical links are underused and often idle. TRILL, in contrast, supports the simultaneous use of multiple equal-cost paths, enabling true load balancing and efficient link utilization. This is particularly valuable in data centers and large-scale networks where traffic volumes are high and predictable performance is essential. TRILL's ability to distribute traffic across multiple paths also improves redundancy and resilience, as failures on one path do not necessitate a complete topology recalculation, as is often the case with spanning tree.

TRILL also introduces faster convergence times by eliminating the dependency on timers and state transitions that characterize spanning tree behavior. In traditional STP environments, when a topology change occurs, switches must wait for timers to expire before activating new paths, resulting in convergence delays of up to 50 seconds in legacy STP and still a few seconds even in RSTP. TRILL, using its link-state routing base, recalculates paths almost instantaneously upon detecting changes in the network. This enables sub-second convergence times, which are critical in environments where application uptime and user experience depend on uninterrupted connectivity.

Compatibility with legacy Ethernet equipment is another reason TRILL is considered an evolution rather than a complete replacement of spanning tree. While TRILL-capable devices form the core of the TRILL domain, traditional Ethernet devices can still connect to the network via edge ports on RBridges. These edge ports translate between TRILL encapsulated frames and standard Ethernet frames, allowing for seamless interoperability. This means that organizations can gradually adopt TRILL in existing networks without requiring a complete overhaul of all infrastructure, preserving investment while gaining the benefits of modern networking capabilities.

The architecture of TRILL also inherently improves network security and stability. Because routing decisions are made based on a controlled, authenticated IS-IS topology database, there is less opportunity for rogue devices to manipulate the forwarding topology by spoofing BPDUs or masquerading as root bridges, as can happen in spanning tree networks. Additionally, the use of a hop count in the TRILL header ensures that packets cannot circulate endlessly in the network, which further reduces the risk of broadcast storms and resource exhaustion due to misconfigurations or malicious attacks.

TRILL's integration with modern technologies, such as virtualized data centers and cloud computing, reinforces its status as an evolved solution. It supports the needs of virtual machine mobility, east-west traffic optimization, and high-density server interconnections without the traditional constraints of spanning tree. It offers a foundation upon which overlay networks and higher-level orchestration tools can function more predictably and performantly. By enabling a scalable, efficient, and resilient fabric, TRILL aligns with the evolving architecture of modern IT environments and paves the way for more agile and automated network designs.

While spanning tree protocols laid the groundwork for safe and structured Layer 2 networking, the demands of modern infrastructure have outgrown their limitations. TRILL emerges not as a radical departure, but as a sophisticated continuation of the original mission of Ethernet loop prevention—achieving a stable, high-performance, and scalable network. By replacing blocking with routing, convergence delays with real-time path recalculations, and flooded learning with intelligent control-plane knowledge, TRILL represents a true evolution of spanning tree, tailored for the data-driven, always-on, and dynamic nature of contemporary networks.

TRILL Control Plane and IS-IS

The TRILL protocol, or Transparent Interconnection of Lots of Links, is fundamentally different from traditional spanning tree-based protocols in that it replaces a passive, timer-based control mechanism with a dynamic, link-state routing model that delivers faster convergence, better loop prevention, and more efficient path utilization. At the core of this new architecture lies its control plane, which is built on the Intermediate System to Intermediate System protocol, more commonly known as IS-IS. The choice of IS-IS as the foundation for TRILL's control plane was not incidental but deliberate, providing the protocol with the robust, scalable, and adaptable capabilities needed for modern Layer 2 networks, particularly in data center environments where speed, redundancy, and intelligent path computation are essential.

IS-IS is a link-state routing protocol traditionally used at Layer 3 in IP networks, especially in service provider backbones due to its efficiency and scalability. What makes IS-IS particularly suitable for TRILL is that it operates directly over Layer 2, without relying on IP addressing for control message exchange. This means TRILL can use IS-IS to distribute topology information and compute shortest paths without needing to assign IP addresses to each interface or maintain Layer 3 adjacency. This attribute simplifies implementation in pure Layer 2 environments while still allowing the benefits of routing logic to be fully realized.

In the TRILL control plane, each Routing Bridge, or RBridge, runs its own IS-IS instance. These RBridges form adjacencies with their directly connected peers by exchanging IS-IS Hello packets. Once adjacencies are established, RBridges begin to exchange Link-State Protocol Data Units, or LSPs, which contain detailed information about the state of their interfaces, the identity of their neighbors, and any reachable destinations. These LSPs are flooded throughout the TRILL network, enabling all RBridges to build a consistent and synchronized topology database, often referred to as the Link-State Database. From this database, each RBridge independently runs the Dijkstra shortest path first algorithm to calculate the most efficient path to every other RBridge in the TRILL domain.

The result of this calculation is a forwarding table that maps each destination RBridge to the appropriate output port. Because all RBridges have the same topology information and use the same algorithm, the network achieves loop-free, consistent, and deterministic forwarding behavior. This contrasts sharply with the behavior of STP-based networks, where convergence is reactive and relies on indirect BPDU propagation and port state transitions, leading to slower recovery from failures and less efficient use of links.

One of the most significant benefits of using IS-IS in the TRILL control plane is its ability to support Equal-Cost Multi-Path routing. Since IS-IS identifies all shortest paths between nodes, TRILL can take advantage of multiple links of equal cost, balancing traffic across them for improved bandwidth utilization and fault tolerance. Traditional spanning tree protocols block redundant links to prevent loops, resulting in wasted capacity. TRILL, powered by the IS-IS control plane, activates all available links and dynamically selects among them based on current topology and cost metrics.

The IS-IS control plane in TRILL also facilitates rapid convergence. Because it maintains a real-time topology database and does not depend on timers for recalculation, the network can react quickly to link failures or topology changes. When an interface goes down, the RBridge immediately updates its LSP and floods this information to all other RBridges. Each device then recalculates its forwarding paths using the updated topology, typically in milliseconds. This real-time responsiveness allows TRILL networks to meet the high availability requirements of mission-critical applications and virtualized data center environments where even brief interruptions can have significant consequences.

IS-IS in TRILL is also extensible, allowing for additional information to be carried alongside traditional link-state data. TRILL uses this extensibility to distribute various types of control information beyond just topology. For instance, TRILL leverages IS-IS to advertise nickname mappings, which are used to identify RBridges in the TRILL header instead of using full MAC addresses. This nickname-based addressing reduces frame overhead and simplifies forwarding logic. The nickname assignment is coordinated among RBridges to ensure uniqueness, and the control plane ensures that all devices remain synchronized.

Another important aspect of the TRILL control plane is the support for VLAN and multicast distribution tree information. While TRILL encapsulates Ethernet frames and forwards them based on RBridge nicknames, it still honors the traditional Ethernet semantics of broadcast, unknown unicast, and multicast traffic. To handle these traffic types efficiently, TRILL uses distribution trees, which are calculated and advertised using IS-IS. Each RBridge designates a root for the distribution tree, and the IS-IS control plane ensures that the tree spans all RBridges in the domain. This method allows for optimized and loop-free flooding, reducing unnecessary traffic replication and ensuring that frames reach all intended recipients.

Security and robustness are also addressed within the TRILL control plane through IS-IS. The protocol supports authentication of LSPs, ensuring that only authorized RBridges participate in the TRILL domain. This prevents rogue devices from injecting false topology information or disrupting the network. Moreover, IS-IS includes mechanisms for graceful restart and link-state pacing, which helps maintain stability and continuity during control plane restarts or temporary disruptions. These features contribute to the operational reliability and trustworthiness of TRILL-based networks.

The separation of control and data planes in TRILL further enhances its flexibility. While IS-IS governs the calculation and dissemination of topology and forwarding information, the actual forwarding of frames is handled independently in the data plane. This modularity allows for more consistent behavior and easier integration with hardware-based forwarding engines. It also enables rapid adaptation to network changes without the need for extensive reprogramming of forwarding paths, as the control plane continually supplies updated information to the data plane in real time.

As networks continue to scale in size and complexity, the role of the TRILL control plane and its reliance on IS-IS become even more critical. The ability to manage thousands of devices and links, compute optimal paths across a dynamic topology, and respond quickly to changes makes this architecture well-suited to meet the demands of modern networking. Whether in a data center fabric, campus backbone, or service provider aggregation layer, TRILL and IS-IS together deliver a powerful combination of agility, efficiency, and stability. Understanding the operation of the TRILL control plane and the role of IS-IS within it is key to designing and operating high-performance Layer 2 networks that are both scalable and resilient.

TRILL Nicknames and Routing Tables

The TRILL protocol introduces a series of innovations that transform the behavior of traditional Layer 2 Ethernet networks by enabling routing-like functionality within the data link layer. Among the most critical elements of this transformation are the use of nicknames and the construction of TRILL routing tables, both of which are essential for the scalability, efficiency, and loop-free operation of TRILL-enabled networks. Unlike classical Ethernet switching that relies on MAC address learning and flooding for frame forwarding, TRILL employs a structured and intelligent forwarding model in which devices make deterministic decisions based on a control-plane-calculated network topology. This model hinges on the assignment of unique nicknames to RBridges and the population of routing tables that govern how frames are forwarded across the TRILL domain.

In a TRILL network, each Routing Bridge, or RBridge, is assigned a two-byte identifier known as a nickname. This nickname serves as a compact representation of the RBridge's identity and is used in the TRILL encapsulation header to indicate both the ingress and egress points for a frame as it travels through the TRILL fabric. The use of nicknames is critical because it reduces the size of the TRILL header, thereby improving efficiency and reducing overhead. If TRILL were to use full MAC addresses in every frame for routing purposes, the protocol would inherit many of the same limitations as traditional Ethernet. Instead, by abstracting MAC addresses and representing each RBridge with a simple nickname, TRILL simplifies forwarding and accelerates lookup processes.

Nicknames are not assigned arbitrarily. The nickname allocation process is managed through the IS-IS control plane, which allows all participating RBridges to announce their desired nicknames and detect any conflicts. Each RBridge claims a nickname and advertises it through its IS-IS Link State PDU. All other RBridges in the TRILL domain receive this information and build a consistent nickname-to-RBridge mapping. In the event of a conflict, where two RBridges attempt to claim the same nickname, the conflict is resolved using a deterministic tie-breaking process that takes into account factors such as the MAC address of the RBridge. This ensures that each nickname is globally unique within the TRILL domain, which is essential for correct frame forwarding and loop avoidance.

The significance of TRILL nicknames becomes apparent when examining the structure of the TRILL data plane. When an Ethernet frame enters the TRILL domain at an ingress RBridge, that RBridge encapsulates the original frame with a TRILL header that includes its own nickname as the ingress identifier and the destination RBridge's nickname as the egress identifier. This encapsulated frame is then forwarded based on the routing tables built from the link-state database. The routing tables contain shortest path information calculated using the Dijkstra algorithm, with each entry mapping a destination nickname to the appropriate outbound interface and next-hop RBridge. Since the TRILL header includes both the source and destination nicknames, each intermediate RBridge can simply consult its table to determine the next step, much like a router would forward an IP packet.

Routing tables in TRILL are maintained per nickname, not per MAC address. This model significantly reduces the complexity of the control plane and the size of forwarding tables in large networks. Instead of tracking the location of every end device by MAC address across the entire topology, RBridges only need to track other RBridges by nickname. MAC address learning is still performed, but it is localized to the edge RBridges, which associate end station MAC addresses with ingress and egress nicknames rather than specific port identifiers. When a frame is destined for a known MAC address, the ingress RBridge simply determines which nickname corresponds to the RBridge that learned the MAC and encapsulates the frame accordingly. This approach enables Layer 2 connectivity while scaling the control plane in a manner that traditional Ethernet cannot achieve.

Another layer of complexity and functionality in TRILL routing tables comes into play with support for Equal-Cost Multi-Path routing. If multiple paths exist to reach a particular nickname with the same cost, the routing table can include multiple next-hop options. The RBridge then selects among these options either through hashing mechanisms or load-balancing algorithms to distribute traffic evenly across all available paths. This multipath capability allows TRILL to fully utilize all links in the network, increasing throughput and providing greater redundancy. The TRILL routing tables are therefore not static but dynamic, adjusting as topology changes occur and link-state updates are received through IS-IS.

The separation of data plane forwarding and control plane topology management ensures that TRILL networks can adapt quickly and recover gracefully from failures. When a link goes down, the affected RBridge updates its IS-IS LSP, and the change is propagated throughout the domain. Each RBridge recalculates its shortest path tree and updates its routing table entries accordingly. Because the entries are keyed by nickname, this recalculation is straightforward and efficient. Frames destined for the affected RBridge will be routed through alternative paths using updated next-hop information, minimizing disruption and maintaining connectivity.

Nicknames also play a role in multicast and unknown unicast forwarding. In TRILL, special distribution trees are created for flooding traffic that does not have a known destination MAC address. These distribution trees are rooted at specific RBridges and calculated in advance using IS-IS. When a frame needs to be flooded, it is encapsulated with the root nickname of the appropriate distribution tree, and forwarding proceeds along that tree. Since the forwarding decisions are based on nicknames rather than flooding all ports like traditional Ethernet, TRILL can flood frames efficiently and without creating loops.

The TRILL protocol's use of nicknames and routing tables represents a significant architectural advancement over the flat and reactive model of Ethernet switching. By introducing a structured and deterministic forwarding paradigm, TRILL achieves the scalability, speed, and redundancy required by modern networks. Nicknames reduce overhead, simplify forwarding logic, and make routing more manageable, while the dynamic, link-state-driven routing tables ensure that traffic is delivered efficiently, even in large and constantly changing topologies. Understanding how these elements interact is essential for designing, implementing, and maintaining high-performance TRILL networks that can meet the evolving demands of cloud computing, virtualization, and high-density data center architectures.

TRILL Encapsulation and Headers

The TRILL protocol fundamentally reimagines how Ethernet frames are transported across Layer 2 networks by introducing encapsulation techniques that mirror the behavior of routing protocols while preserving Ethernet semantics. At the core of this approach lies the TRILL encapsulation header, a construct that enables frames to be routed intelligently through a fabric of Routing Bridges, or RBridges, using shortest-path logic rather than traditional flooding and learning mechanisms. TRILL encapsulation and headers are critical to understanding the way the protocol delivers scalability, multipathing, and loop prevention while remaining compatible with existing Ethernet infrastructure.

When a frame enters a TRILL-enabled network, it is received by an ingress RBridge, which examines the destination MAC address to determine whether the destination is within the TRILL domain. If the destination is located within the TRILL fabric, the ingress RBridge encapsulates the original Ethernet frame in a TRILL header. This encapsulated frame is then forwarded through the network based on information learned from the IS-IS control plane, which calculates optimal paths between RBridges using a link-state algorithm. This encapsulation marks the transition from traditional Ethernet behavior to TRILL's more advanced routing-like methodology, allowing the network to scale and converge faster than legacy spanning tree designs.

The TRILL header is inserted between the original Ethernet header and the new outer Ethernet header, creating a three-part structure for encapsulated frames. The inner Ethernet frame remains intact, preserving the original source and destination MAC addresses, VLAN tags, and payload. This ensures compatibility with standard Ethernet devices and services at the network edges. The TRILL header adds metadata that allows the frame to be routed intelligently through the TRILL domain. Finally, the outer Ethernet header is constructed by the ingress RBridge for delivery to the next-hop RBridge, allowing the frame to be transported from RBridge to RBridge like a Layer 3 packet between routers.

The TRILL header itself contains several fields that define how the frame should be handled by intermediate RBridges. One of the most important fields is the egress RBridge nickname. This two-byte value identifies the RBridge responsible for delivering the frame to its final destination. Because TRILL does not require each switch to track the location of every MAC address in the network, the use of nicknames greatly simplifies forwarding decisions and reduces control plane overhead. Instead of mapping MAC addresses to output ports as in traditional Ethernet, RBridges forward encapsulated frames based on the egress nickname using their TRILL routing tables.

The TRILL header also contains the ingress RBridge nickname. This field allows intermediate RBridges and the egress RBridge to identify the origin of the encapsulated frame. In addition to supporting diagnostics and troubleshooting, the ingress nickname is used by the egress RBridge to update MAC address tables and to learn the mapping between MAC addresses and the corresponding ingress RBridge. This learning process allows subsequent return traffic to be efficiently routed without the need for flooding, further enhancing the scalability of the network.

Another critical component of the TRILL header is the hop count. This value is initialized by the ingress RBridge and decremented by each RBridge along the forwarding path. The inclusion of a hop count provides a safeguard against routing loops, ensuring that a frame cannot circulate indefinitely in the network. If the hop count reaches zero before the frame arrives at the egress RBridge, the frame is discarded. This behavior mirrors the Time-To-Live mechanism found in IP networks and represents a fundamental improvement over traditional Ethernet, where looping frames can persist until link buffers are exhausted, causing broadcast storms and network outages.

The TRILL header also includes various control bits and flags that guide forwarding behavior. One such bit indicates whether the frame should be forwarded using a distribution tree, which is necessary for multicast, broadcast, and unknown unicast traffic. When this bit is set, the frame is forwarded along a precomputed tree rooted at a specific RBridge. The TRILL header includes the root nickname of this tree, ensuring that all RBridges in the domain forward the frame consistently and without creating loops. This tree-based forwarding model allows TRILL to replicate the necessary aspects of traditional Ethernet flooding while maintaining the deterministic and loop-free characteristics of routing.

Encapsulated TRILL frames also feature an outer Ethernet header used for hop-by-hop delivery between RBridges. This header includes the source MAC address of the current sending RBridge and the destination MAC address of the receiving RBridge. Because TRILL uses standard Ethernet frames for transport between RBridges, it can be deployed in existing Ethernet networks and over conventional Ethernet switches that do not participate in the TRILL control plane. This compatibility is a key advantage of TRILL, allowing for gradual deployment and integration into mixed environments without the need for a complete infrastructure overhaul.

One important consideration in TRILL encapsulation is the impact on Maximum Transmission Unit (MTU). The addition of the TRILL and outer Ethernet headers increases the size of the frame, potentially exceeding the MTU on some links. Network designers must ensure that links within the TRILL domain support a sufficient MTU, typically referred to as jumbo frames, to accommodate the additional overhead. Failure to account for MTU requirements can lead to fragmentation or dropped frames, reducing network performance and reliability.

The decapsulation process occurs at the egress RBridge, where the TRILL header and outer Ethernet header are stripped, and the original Ethernet frame is delivered to the final destination. From the perspective of the end host, this delivery is indistinguishable from a standard Ethernet transmission. The transparency of the encapsulation and decapsulation processes is critical to TRILL's design, ensuring seamless interoperability with existing applications and network devices while enabling the internal network to operate with the efficiency and intelligence of a routed topology.

TRILL encapsulation and its associated headers provide the structural foundation for many of the protocol's advanced capabilities. By encapsulating Ethernet frames with routing metadata, TRILL bridges the gap between the simplicity of Layer 2 forwarding and the intelligence of Layer 3 routing. This model enables TRILL networks to scale, converge quickly, and utilize all available paths without the risk of loops or broadcast storms. Understanding the mechanics of TRILL encapsulation and the function of each header field is essential for designing, deploying, and troubleshooting TRILL-enabled networks, especially in environments where performance, reliability, and scalability are of paramount importance.

Multi-Destination Frames in TRILL

In traditional Ethernet networks, multi-destination frames, which include broadcast, multicast, and unknown unicast frames, are delivered through a flooding mechanism that replicates packets across all relevant ports within a broadcast domain. This approach, while simple, introduces scalability and performance challenges in larger networks, where excessive flooding can lead to broadcast storms, wasted bandwidth, and inefficient use of resources. The Transparent Interconnection of Lots of Links (TRILL) protocol offers a more sophisticated mechanism for handling multi-destination traffic. Rather than relying on indiscriminate flooding, TRILL uses precomputed distribution trees to deliver multi-destination frames efficiently and loop-free across a Layer 2 fabric that behaves more like a routed infrastructure.

Multi-destination traffic in TRILL is handled through a concept known as distribution trees. These are loop-free paths spanning the entire TRILL domain and are rooted at specific RBridges. When a frame classified as broadcast, multicast, or unknown unicast enters the TRILL domain, the ingress RBridge encapsulates it with a TRILL header that indicates the root of the distribution tree to be used for forwarding. The tree is selected based on load balancing strategies, network design preferences, or administrative configuration. Each intermediate RBridge in the network, upon receiving the frame, consults its topology database and forwards the frame to all downstream branches of the tree, ensuring that the frame reaches every part of the network that is part of the tree while avoiding loops or duplicate deliveries.

The creation of distribution trees relies on the IS-IS link-state protocol used by TRILL for its control plane. Each RBridge advertises its connectivity to neighbors and its capability to serve as a distribution tree root. Based on these advertisements, all RBridges in the network independently compute identical tree topologies using the Dijkstra algorithm. This ensures consistency in forwarding behavior, as every RBridge understands how to forward a multi-destination frame that is associated with a particular root. The root of the tree is represented by the nickname of the RBridge, which is inserted into the TRILL header during encapsulation. By centralizing the tree construction through IS-IS but allowing for distributed computation, TRILL ensures resilience and synchronization without centralized control.

Unknown unicast traffic, which arises when the destination MAC address is not present in the forwarding database of the ingress RBridge, is also treated as multi-destination traffic in TRILL. The frame is forwarded along a distribution tree to reach all RBridges, under the assumption that one of them will recognize the MAC address. When the correct RBridge receives the frame and identifies the destination MAC as locally attached, it decapsulates the frame and delivers it to the endpoint. This process also enables MAC learning. The egress RBridge informs the network about the mapping between the MAC address and the ingress nickname, allowing future frames to be sent directly without requiring flooding.

Multicast traffic in TRILL is handled with similar efficiency. Instead of flooding multicast frames to every switch in the domain, TRILL supports the registration of multicast listeners and optimizes delivery through pruning mechanisms. RBridges can learn which end devices have expressed interest in particular multicast groups and limit the replication of frames to only those parts of the tree that lead to interested receivers. This intelligent pruning reduces unnecessary load on links and devices that do not require the multicast traffic. It also aligns TRILL with IP multicast behavior, where multicast routing protocols selectively forward traffic based on group membership. This feature is particularly valuable in environments where video streaming, conferencing, or other multicast-dependent applications are in use.

Broadcast frames, while relatively rare in well-designed networks, are still supported in TRILL. These include Address Resolution Protocol (ARP) requests, DHCP discovery messages, and certain network announcements. When such frames are received by an ingress RBridge, they are forwarded across a distribution tree just like other multi-destination frames. The tree-based approach ensures that the frame is delivered to all nodes in the TRILL domain while preventing loops and duplicate reception. Because TRILL's control plane ensures that only a single copy of the broadcast frame reaches each destination, the risk of broadcast storms is minimized, even in topologies with many redundant paths.

Load balancing of multi-destination traffic is achieved in TRILL through the use of multiple distribution trees. A network may designate several RBridges as potential roots and compute separate trees for each. The ingress RBridge can select from these trees to distribute traffic more evenly across the network fabric. This selection may be random, round-robin, or based on VLAN groupings or other policies. By using different trees for different streams or types of traffic, TRILL avoids concentrating all multi-destination traffic on a single set of links, increasing the overall throughput and reliability of the fabric. It also allows the network to adapt to failures more gracefully, as alternate trees can be used in the event of congestion or link loss.

One of the most significant benefits of TRILL's approach to multi-destination frames is its deterministic behavior. Unlike traditional Ethernet flooding, which is subject to variability and imprecision, TRILL's use of IS-IS-computed distribution trees ensures that every RBridge forwards frames in a predictable and controlled manner. This deterministic behavior simplifies network design, monitoring, and troubleshooting. Network administrators can trace the exact path of a multi-destination frame through the distribution tree and verify that replication and forwarding behaviors conform to the intended topology.

The efficiency of multi-destination forwarding in TRILL also translates into better scalability. In very large Ethernet networks, traditional flooding mechanisms become untenable due to the sheer volume of broadcast and unknown unicast traffic. TRILL mitigates this issue by reducing the scope of flooding and ensuring that only the necessary RBridges handle each frame. This controlled replication reduces pressure on switch CPUs, forwarding engines, and link bandwidth, enabling the network to support more devices, more VLANs, and more applications without degradation in performance.

TRILL's treatment of multi-destination frames exemplifies the protocol's hybrid nature. It preserves the core functional requirements of Ethernet—broadcast delivery, multicast support, and unknown unicast forwarding—while applying the rigor and intelligence of routed networks to these tasks. By using distribution trees, TRILL enables the reliable delivery of frames to multiple destinations without the inefficiencies and risks associated with traditional Ethernet flooding. As networks grow in size and complexity, this capability becomes increasingly important for maintaining service quality, ensuring predictable performance, and supporting the diverse communication patterns that modern applications demand. Understanding how TRILL handles multi-destination frames is essential for designing networks that are not only resilient and scalable but also optimized for the kinds of traffic that define today's connected environments.

Comparing TRILL to Traditional STP

The evolution of network design has consistently been driven by the pursuit of higher performance, improved redundancy, and more scalable topologies. At the core of this evolution in Layer 2 networking is the transition from the Spanning Tree Protocol to more advanced mechanisms like the Transparent Interconnection of Lots of Links, or TRILL. These two protocols represent fundamentally different approaches to solving the problem of loops and redundancy in Ethernet networks. Traditional STP has long been the default solution for ensuring loop-free Layer 2 environments, while TRILL was developed as a response to the growing limitations of STP in large, modern networks. A comparison between the two reveals a clear shift from reactive, timer-driven topology management to proactive, path-optimized forwarding enabled by routing intelligence at Layer 2.

STP, as defined by IEEE 802.1D, operates by calculating a single spanning tree across the network and blocking any redundant paths that could form loops. This results in a loop-free topology but also means that many links remain idle and cannot be used for forwarding traffic. Redundant paths exist only for failover and provide no benefit during normal operation. This inefficiency becomes increasingly problematic as networks scale, particularly in data centers or large campus environments where bandwidth demands are high and the need for resiliency is constant. TRILL addresses this issue by eliminating the need to block paths. It allows all links to be active and uses a routing protocol to determine the shortest path for frame forwarding. By doing so, TRILL achieves full utilization of the available topology, enabling load balancing and higher throughput.

Another significant difference between STP and TRILL lies in convergence behavior. When a topology change occurs in an STP network, such as a link failure or a switch reboot, the protocol must recalculate the spanning tree. This process involves timer-based transitions through listening and learning states before a port can move into the forwarding state. Even with enhancements like Rapid Spanning Tree Protocol, convergence can still take seconds, which is unacceptable in environments where uptime and real-time data flow are critical. TRILL, on the other hand, relies on the IS-IS link-state routing protocol, which rapidly disseminates topology changes to all participating RBridges. Each RBridge then independently recalculates the shortest paths using Dijkstra's algorithm. The result is sub-second convergence times and a network that can adapt quickly to failures without disrupting ongoing traffic.

Scalability is another area where TRILL significantly outperforms STP. In traditional STP networks, every switch must participate in a single spanning tree, and all broadcast domains are flat. This model limits the number of devices and VLANs that can be efficiently managed and leads to performance bottlenecks as the network grows. STP also depends heavily on MAC address learning and flooding, which adds to the burden on switch resources. TRILL introduces a hierarchical model using RBridges, nicknames, and routing tables that significantly reduces control plane overhead. Rather than tracking every MAC address across the entire network, TRILL switches only maintain mappings between MAC addresses and their associated ingress or egress RBridges. The use of nicknames and TRILL headers enables efficient forwarding decisions without the need for widespread flooding or large MAC tables, allowing the network to scale with far greater efficiency.

Another point of comparison is the way each protocol handles multi-destination traffic. In STP, broadcast, multicast, and unknown unicast frames are flooded across all ports in the spanning tree except the one they were received on. This can lead to excessive replication of frames and congestion on the network, especially in large topologies. TRILL handles multi-destination traffic using precomputed distribution trees rooted at specific RBridges. These trees provide a loop-free, optimized path for forwarding multi-destination frames, reducing unnecessary replication and ensuring that each frame reaches its intended recipients only once. This design leads to more predictable network behavior and better use of available bandwidth.

Loop prevention mechanisms are also fundamentally different. STP prevents loops by blocking redundant links, which reduces path availability. It relies on periodic BPDUs and the election of a root bridge, with the entire topology structured around this single logical root. This model introduces a single point of dependency and can result in suboptimal path selection. TRILL avoids loops through a combination of hop count in the TRILL header and the inherent loop-free nature of the link-state routing protocol it uses. Since every RBridge knows the full topology and calculates routes accordingly, loops are inherently avoided, and traffic takes the shortest path to its destination. The inclusion of a hop count in the TRILL encapsulation provides additional protection against looping frames, which is particularly important in complex topologies with multiple equal-cost paths.

Deployment and interoperability further highlight the differences. STP is well-supported across virtually all Ethernet devices and requires minimal configuration, making it a simple and widely compatible solution. However, its simplicity comes at the cost of performance and scalability. TRILL is a more advanced protocol that requires RBridge-capable devices and support for IS-IS. While it introduces greater complexity, it also brings a more powerful feature set. TRILL can coexist with legacy Ethernet devices at the edge of the network, allowing organizations to deploy it incrementally without a full infrastructure replacement. This backward compatibility, combined with its advanced capabilities, makes TRILL a practical upgrade path for networks struggling with the limitations of spanning tree.

Security and traffic isolation also benefit from TRILL's architectural improvements. In STP networks, it is possible for misconfigured or malicious devices to influence the topology by sending forged BPDUs, potentially becoming the root bridge and disrupting traffic flows. STP does not authenticate BPDUs by default, making the protocol vulnerable to manipulation. TRILL leverages IS-IS authentication mechanisms and does not use BPDUs, making it more secure against certain types of attacks. The use of a controlled control plane and hop-by-hop forwarding based on trusted nicknames enhances both security and predictability.

In essence, the comparison between STP and TRILL reflects the broader shift in networking from static, reactive designs to dynamic, intelligent architectures. While STP remains a valid solution for small or simple environments, its limitations in performance, convergence, and scalability make it less suitable for the demands of modern networks. TRILL, by introducing routing logic into Layer 2, redefines what is possible within an Ethernet fabric. It offers faster convergence, better path utilization, support for multipathing, improved handling of broadcast and multicast traffic, and enhanced scalability. These features collectively position TRILL as a natural and necessary evolution of traditional spanning tree protocols, especially in data center and high-density campus networks where performance and reliability are non-negotiable. Understanding these differences is essential for network architects seeking to build next-generation infrastructures that meet the expectations of speed, efficiency, and resilience.

TRILL Convergence and Path Selection

The convergence behavior and path selection mechanism in TRILL, the Transparent Interconnection of Lots of Links protocol, mark a fundamental departure from traditional Layer 2 Ethernet protocols. Unlike the Spanning Tree Protocol, which relies on a centralized, timer-driven process to prevent loops and select forwarding paths, TRILL leverages the power of distributed link-state routing to determine the shortest and most efficient path through a Layer 2 network. This shift enables TRILL to deliver fast convergence, intelligent traffic distribution, and greater overall network performance. At the heart of TRILL's convergence capabilities lies its use of the IS-IS routing protocol, which provides a synchronized and real-time view of the network topology to all Routing Bridges, or RBridges. These features allow TRILL networks to quickly adapt to topology changes, reroute traffic with minimal disruption, and fully utilize available bandwidth through multipath routing.

In a TRILL network, convergence begins with the initial discovery of network topology. Each RBridge forms adjacencies with its directly connected neighbors by exchanging IS-IS Hello packets. Once these adjacencies are established, the RBridges begin to exchange Link State Protocol Data Units containing information about their interfaces, connected neighbors, and reachable destinations. These link-state advertisements are flooded throughout the TRILL domain, allowing every RBridge to independently build a complete map of the network. This topology map is stored in the Link State Database and serves as the foundation for all subsequent path calculations. The use of a link-state protocol like IS-IS ensures that all RBridges have a consistent view of the network at all times, which is essential for fast and accurate convergence.

When a change in the network occurs, such as a link failure, new RBridge joining, or topology reconfiguration, the affected RBridge immediately generates a new link-state advertisement reflecting the change. This update is propagated to all other RBridges in the network. Because each RBridge maintains its own instance of the link-state database, they can each independently recompute the shortest path tree using Dijkstra's algorithm. This distributed approach to convergence eliminates the need for timers or hierarchical root selection, which are central to spanning tree protocols. Instead, TRILL offers event-driven convergence, allowing the network to adapt to changes in milliseconds rather than waiting for predefined intervals to expire.

Path selection in TRILL is determined by the results of the shortest path computation, which calculates the lowest-cost route from the current RBridge to every other RBridge in the domain. Cost in this context can refer to link metrics such as bandwidth, delay, or administrative preferences. The result of this calculation is a routing table that maps destination RBridge nicknames to specific output interfaces. Because each RBridge performs this calculation independently but based on the same data, the resulting forwarding decisions are consistent and loop-free. This predictability enhances the stability of the network and ensures that frames follow the optimal path to their destination.

One of the major advantages of TRILL's path selection model is its support for Equal-Cost Multi-Path routing, or ECMP. When multiple paths exist between two RBridges with the same cost, TRILL can load-balance traffic across these paths. This feature significantly increases the network's ability to use all available links simultaneously, as opposed to traditional spanning tree protocols which block all but one path to avoid loops. By distributing traffic across equal-cost paths, TRILL not only increases available bandwidth but also improves resilience. If one path fails, traffic can continue flowing over the remaining paths without requiring a complete reconvergence of the topology. This dynamic and efficient use of network resources is a key benefit of TRILL's architecture.

TRILL also makes use of nicknames, which are unique two-byte identifiers assigned to each RBridge. These nicknames simplify the path selection and forwarding process by allowing RBridges to build their routing tables based on short identifiers rather than full MAC addresses. When an Ethernet frame enters the TRILL domain, the ingress RBridge encapsulates it with a TRILL header containing the destination nickname. The intermediate RBridges forward the frame based on their routing tables until it reaches the egress RBridge, which decapsulates the frame and delivers it to the final destination. The use of nicknames reduces control plane complexity, speeds up lookups, and supports better scalability by minimizing the size of routing tables.

To maintain loop-free operation, TRILL employs a hop count mechanism in the TRILL header, similar to the TTL field in IP packets. Each time a frame is forwarded by an RBridge, the hop count is decremented. If the hop count reaches zero before the frame reaches its destination, the frame is discarded. This ensures that even in the event of a misconfiguration or temporary routing inconsistency, frames do not endlessly circulate in the network. Combined with the link-state nature of IS-IS, the hop count provides a secondary layer of protection against loops and ensures that all traffic is routed safely and efficiently.

Convergence and path selection are further enhanced in TRILL by its support for multiple distribution trees, particularly for handling multi-destination frames such as broadcasts, multicasts, and unknown unicasts. Each RBridge can be configured to serve as the root of one or more distribution trees. When a frame requires flooding, the ingress RBridge selects a distribution tree and encapsulates the frame accordingly. The intermediate RBridges forward the frame along the branches of the selected tree, ensuring that it reaches all intended recipients while avoiding loops. These trees are also calculated using the same IS-IS link-state data and provide a structured and deterministic approach to multi-destination traffic delivery.

Fast convergence and intelligent path selection are crucial in modern networks where downtime is costly and user experience is paramount. TRILL's architecture allows it to respond instantly to changes, using prebuilt routing logic and distributed computation to reestablish connectivity. This capability is particularly important in virtualized and cloud-based environments, where workloads may move between physical locations, and the network must adapt on the fly. With TRILL, traffic paths can shift immediately in response to these changes, maintaining optimal performance and minimizing latency.

In contrast to spanning tree-based networks, which often react slowly and inefficiently to changes, TRILL offers a proactive and performance-driven solution. Its convergence model is not tied to the constraints of loop-avoidance through port blocking but instead leverages real-time topology awareness to enable flexible and resilient forwarding. This empowers network designers to build topologies that are both redundant and fully active, breaking free from the traditional limitations of Ethernet switching. Through its sophisticated use of IS-IS, nickname-based forwarding, and dynamic path recalculation, TRILL represents a leap forward in Layer 2 networking, bringing the benefits of routing to environments that still rely on Ethernet for fundamental connectivity. Understanding TRILL's convergence behavior and path selection mechanisms is essential for deploying high-performance networks capable of supporting the demands of modern applications, services, and architectures.

TRILL and Equal Cost Multipath

Equal Cost Multipath, or ECMP, is a critical capability in modern network design that allows for the use of multiple active paths with the same cost between a source and destination. In traditional Ethernet environments governed by spanning tree-based protocols, this type of path redundancy is unavailable because the protocol must block redundant paths to prevent loops. As a result, only one path is used while all others remain idle, leading to inefficient use of available bandwidth and underutilized infrastructure. TRILL, or Transparent Interconnection of Lots of Links, fundamentally changes this paradigm by integrating ECMP capabilities directly into its forwarding logic. This enables the network to simultaneously utilize multiple paths of equal cost, resulting in better load balancing, increased fault tolerance, and significantly improved overall performance.

TRILL accomplishes ECMP through its use of a link-state routing protocol, IS-IS, which provides each Routing Bridge with a complete view of the topology. All RBridges in the network participate in this control plane and share link-state information through a series of IS-IS advertisements. Each RBridge constructs an identical link-state database and independently calculates the shortest path to every other RBridge using Dijkstra's algorithm. In cases where multiple shortest paths exist between a pair of RBridges, TRILL recognizes these as equal-cost paths. Rather than choosing only one path and ignoring the others, TRILL includes all of them in the forwarding decision, enabling the network to actively balance traffic across multiple routes.

The TRILL protocol relies on nicknames to represent RBridges in the control and data planes. When an Ethernet frame enters the TRILL domain, the ingress RBridge assigns the appropriate egress nickname to the frame based on the destination MAC address. The TRILL header encapsulates the original frame, including both ingress and egress nicknames. The encapsulated frame is then forwarded according to the routing table generated from the IS-IS topology information. When multiple paths of equal cost exist for the egress nickname, the ingress or intermediate RBridge can select among those paths using a deterministic or hash-based algorithm, ensuring even distribution of traffic.

This ability to use multiple paths in parallel improves the network's resiliency. Should one of the paths fail due to a link or node outage, TRILL does not need to perform a major topology recalculation or wait for timers to expire, as in spanning tree-based systems. Instead, the IS-IS protocol quickly updates the topology database, and each RBridge recomputes its path table to exclude the failed component. Since alternative paths are already known and available, convergence occurs rapidly and transparently, maintaining service continuity and minimizing disruption. This fast failover behavior is one of the defining strengths of ECMP in TRILL networks.

From a traffic engineering perspective, TRILL and ECMP offer significant flexibility. Network architects can design topologies with multiple redundant paths, confident that TRILL will use all available bandwidth effectively. Unlike spanning tree, where the physical topology must be designed to avoid blocking desirable links, TRILL allows the network to be built with redundancy and high-capacity interconnects in mind. The protocol takes full advantage of these links without manual intervention, and it dynamically adapts to changes in traffic load and link availability. This is especially beneficial in data center environments where east-west traffic is prevalent, and balanced throughput across aggregation and core layers is essential to maintaining application performance.

TRILL's ECMP capability also reduces the risk of traffic bottlenecks. By spreading flows across several paths, it prevents any single link from becoming overloaded while others remain underutilized. This distribution is typically performed using a hash of various fields in the frame, such as source and destination MAC addresses, VLAN tags, or even Layer 4 information if available. The result is that traffic is divided in a way that maintains the integrity of flow-based communication while maximizing use of the physical infrastructure. This ensures consistent and predictable performance, even as traffic patterns shift due to workload changes, virtual machine migrations, or other dynamic factors.

Load balancing across equal-cost paths can be implemented at different points in the TRILL network. The ingress RBridge has the most visibility into the traffic it is injecting into the TRILL domain and can make initial decisions about which path to use. Intermediate RBridges, depending on their local routing tables, may also have multiple options for forwarding a given frame and can independently decide how to distribute traffic further. This distributed decision-making allows the network to scale efficiently, as no single device becomes a bottleneck or point of failure for path selection. Moreover, because all RBridges share the same view of the topology, their decisions remain consistent, avoiding routing loops or misdirected frames.

ECMP in TRILL does not interfere with the delivery of multi-destination traffic such as broadcasts or multicasts. These traffic types are handled using distribution trees that span the TRILL domain and are rooted at specific RBridges. The use of ECMP applies only to unicast traffic, where multiple equal-cost unicast routes can be used simultaneously. This distinction ensures that each type of traffic is handled by the most appropriate mechanism, optimizing both efficiency and delivery correctness. Unicast traffic benefits from parallel pathing and dynamic load balancing, while multicast and broadcast frames are distributed along calculated trees to reach all intended recipients without duplication or loops.

Another advantage of TRILL's ECMP implementation is its compatibility with modern hardware and high-performance switching architectures. Many network devices support hardware-based hashing and load balancing, enabling them to forward packets across multiple links at line rate. TRILL aligns naturally with these capabilities by providing the control-plane intelligence needed to identify equal-cost paths and the data-plane encapsulation to route frames accordingly. This synergy between control and data planes ensures that TRILL networks can deliver high throughput and low latency, making them ideal for applications such as cloud computing, virtual desktop infrastructure, and large-scale storage fabrics.

The ability to use ECMP also helps simplify network operations. Network administrators do not need to manually tune spanning tree parameters, prune VLANs, or manage complex port roles to achieve balanced utilization. Instead, TRILL handles path selection dynamically and automatically, freeing up operational resources and reducing the risk of human error. Troubleshooting is also simplified, as ECMP decisions are based on predictable hash algorithms and known topology data, making it easier to trace flows and diagnose performance issues.

Ultimately, TRILL's integration of Equal Cost Multipath provides a level of intelligence and efficiency at Layer 2 that was previously only possible with Layer 3 protocols. By enabling multiple active paths, improving convergence, and balancing load dynamically, TRILL enhances network resilience and performance while retaining the flexibility and compatibility of Ethernet. In environments where demand for bandwidth and reliability continues to grow, ECMP within TRILL ensures that networks can scale gracefully and support increasingly complex and data-intensive workloads with confidence. Understanding how TRILL leverages ECMP is essential for designing robust and high-performing Layer 2 topologies that meet the needs of modern enterprises and service providers alike.

Security Considerations in TRILL Networks

As TRILL, or Transparent Interconnection of Lots of Links, brings advanced routing capabilities to Layer 2 Ethernet networks, it also introduces a new set of security considerations that must be carefully understood and addressed to ensure a safe and resilient environment.

TRILL enhances performance and scalability by replacing the traditional spanning tree model with link-state routing and intelligent path selection, but with this shift comes the need for robust mechanisms to protect the control plane, data plane, and network endpoints from potential threats. The distributed nature of TRILL, its reliance on IS-IS for topology information exchange, and the encapsulation of frames with TRILL headers all present unique security implications that differ from those of legacy Ethernet switching.

One of the primary security concerns in a TRILL-enabled network is the integrity of the control plane. TRILL relies on the IS-IS protocol to maintain a synchronized and up-to-date view of the network topology across all Routing Bridges, or RBridges. If an attacker is able to inject false link-state information into the control plane, the consequences could be severe, including traffic redirection, denial of service, or the creation of loops and black holes. To prevent unauthorized participation in the control plane, TRILL mandates the use of authentication for IS-IS link-state advertisements. Each IS-IS packet exchanged between RBridges can be cryptographically authenticated using a shared secret, ensuring that only trusted devices are allowed to influence the topology. Proper key management, regular key rotation, and secure storage of credentials are all essential to maintaining the integrity of this authentication mechanism.

Another area of concern is the potential for rogue RBridges to join the TRILL domain. A malicious device that manages to masquerade as an RBridge could disrupt normal forwarding behavior by advertising bogus nicknames, claiming non-existent links, or attempting to become the root of a distribution tree. To prevent such scenarios, TRILL networks should enforce strict device admission policies at the edge. Port-based access controls such as 802.1X, MAC authentication, or certificate-based validation can be used to ensure that only authorized switches can join the TRILL control plane. Furthermore, network administrators should carefully monitor the list of nicknames and associated RBridge identities to detect anomalies or sudden changes that may indicate the presence of a rogue participant.

TRILL's use of nicknames for forwarding introduces another vector for attack if not properly safeguarded. Since each RBridge is assigned a unique two-byte nickname used in the TRILL header to represent source and destination nodes, the spoofing of these nicknames could lead to incorrect forwarding or eavesdropping. An attacker that successfully impersonates a legitimate RBridge's nickname could receive traffic intended for another device or cause frames to be misrouted. To mitigate this risk, TRILL networks must monitor for nickname conflicts and ensure that the IS-IS control plane enforces uniqueness. Most TRILL implementations resolve conflicts through deterministic tie-breaking rules based on system identifiers, but proactive monitoring and alerting help ensure that nickname inconsistencies are quickly detected and resolved.

Protection of the data plane is equally important. Although TRILL uses encapsulation to forward frames between RBridges, it is still susceptible to traditional Layer 2 attacks such as MAC flooding and address spoofing. In a MAC flooding attack, an adversary injects a large number of bogus source MAC addresses into the network in an attempt to exhaust the RBridges' forwarding tables. When the tables overflow, the switch may resort to flooding frames for unknown destinations, creating opportunities for interception or traffic analysis. To defend against this, TRILL-capable switches should implement MAC limiting, rate-limiting, and anomaly detection to identify and suppress abnormal MAC address activity. Limiting the number of learned MAC addresses per port can prevent individual endpoints from overwhelming the control plane.

Address spoofing, where an attacker forges the source MAC address of legitimate devices, can also disrupt communications and enable man-in-the-middle attacks. TRILL networks should support features like dynamic ARP inspection and DHCP snooping to validate the integrity of Layer 2 to Layer 3 mappings. By ensuring that only expected MAC and IP address pairings are permitted, the network can enforce tighter control over the legitimacy of traffic sources and destinations. Integration with higher-layer security tools such as firewalls and intrusion detection systems further enhances this defense-in-depth approach.

One of TRILL's unique security benefits over traditional spanning tree is its elimination of BPDUs, or Bridge Protocol Data Units, which are commonly exploited in STP-based networks. In STP, malicious BPDUs can be sent by rogue devices to force a topology change, assume the role of the root bridge, or disable key forwarding paths. TRILL's architecture does not use BPDUs, relying instead on IS-IS messaging authenticated at the link level. This change significantly reduces the surface area for certain types of attacks and eliminates the class of threats that depend on manipulating the spanning tree state.

Despite its advantages, TRILL still requires strong operational discipline to maintain a secure posture. Network segmentation using VLANs or VRFs can help isolate critical services and minimize the scope of compromise in the event of a breach. In multi-tenant environments, each tenant should be assigned its own logical segment, and inter-segment communication should be tightly controlled and monitored. Furthermore, TRILL domains must be carefully defined and restricted to known and trusted boundaries. Interfacing with legacy Ethernet or non-TRILL devices should be done through controlled edge ports where standard security controls such as ACLs, inspection, and filtering are in place.

Monitoring and visibility are essential components of TRILL network security. Administrators should deploy telemetry and logging systems that capture IS-IS updates, TRILL encapsulation statistics, and MAC learning events. These logs can be analyzed in real time or archived for forensic purposes, enabling teams to detect suspicious behavior, trace the origin of anomalous packets, and verify compliance with security policies. Integration with network access control systems and SIEM platforms allows TRILL networks to participate in broader enterprise security frameworks, ensuring alignment with organizational standards and best practices.

Physical security must not be overlooked. The most robust control-plane protections are rendered useless if an attacker can gain physical access to a switch or RBridge. All devices participating in the TRILL fabric must be housed in secure environments, with access restricted to authorized personnel. Tamper detection, port security, and physical alarms complement logical defenses to form a comprehensive security architecture.

Securing a TRILL network involves addressing challenges at multiple layers. From authenticating control-plane messages and enforcing nickname uniqueness to defending against data-plane threats and ensuring physical protection, each component plays a role in creating a trustworthy and resilient network. TRILL's design inherently improves upon many weaknesses of traditional Ethernet switching, but it still demands careful planning, consistent monitoring, and strong operational practices to deliver a secure and high-performing Layer 2 environment. As organizations increasingly rely on agile, scalable, and high-availability networks, understanding and implementing the security considerations of TRILL becomes essential to maintaining the confidentiality, integrity, and availability of the services that run on top of it.

Deploying TRILL in Existing Infrastructures

Introducing TRILL, or Transparent Interconnection of Lots of Links, into an existing network infrastructure offers a path toward improved scalability, efficient Layer 2 routing, and enhanced fault tolerance without requiring a complete redesign of the underlying architecture. One of the greatest strengths of TRILL lies in its ability to coexist with traditional Ethernet technologies, including legacy switches running spanning tree protocols such as STP or RSTP. This backward compatibility allows organizations to gradually adopt TRILL as part of a strategic upgrade path, aligning their networks with modern demands for agility and performance while preserving investment in existing hardware and configurations. Deploying TRILL in an operational environment, however, requires a thoughtful plan that considers topology design, device compatibility, protocol interoperability, and the long-term vision for network services.

The first step in integrating TRILL into an established network is identifying suitable segments of the topology where its benefits can be maximized. Core and aggregation layers in data centers and campus networks are particularly well suited to TRILL because they often serve as the backbone for large volumes of east-west traffic. In these layers, the performance improvements gained through multipathing, fast convergence, and better bandwidth utilization can deliver immediate operational value. TRILL-capable switches, known as Routing Bridges or RBridges, are introduced at these points, where they form the foundation of the new TRILL domain. Their deployment is often incremental, beginning with a few interconnected RBridges that participate in the TRILL control plane while maintaining compatibility with downstream devices that continue to use traditional Ethernet switching.

Coexistence between TRILL and legacy STP-based networks is made possible through the concept of TRILL edge ports. These ports, located on the RBridges, serve as interfaces to non-TRILL devices and translate between the TRILL encapsulated frames used internally and the standard Ethernet frames used externally. From the perspective of the legacy devices, the TRILL domain appears as a single bridged segment, meaning that STP operations outside the TRILL network continue unaffected. RBridges automatically detect whether a neighboring device is TRILL-aware or not and adjust their behavior accordingly. This ensures that BPDUs are correctly processed, loops are avoided, and traffic is forwarded in a manner that maintains overall network stability.

When introducing TRILL, careful attention must be given to the formation of the IS-IS control plane. Each RBridge uses IS-IS to advertise its links and compute shortest paths through the TRILL domain. It is important that all participating RBridges are configured with consistent parameters, including authentication settings and nickname allocations. The nickname, a unique two-byte identifier, is used in the TRILL header for routing encapsulated frames. Ensuring nickname uniqueness and resolving any conflicts quickly is essential to preserving correct forwarding behavior. For networks with an existing IS-IS infrastructure used at Layer 3, TRILL operates on a separate instance, preventing interference between the two planes and allowing Layer 2 and Layer 3 routing to coexist harmoniously.

Integration with VLANs and Layer 2 services also requires planning. While TRILL supports VLAN tagging and carries VLAN information within the TRILL header, administrators must decide how VLANs will be extended across the TRILL fabric and how multicast or broadcast traffic will be handled. TRILL computes multicast distribution trees rooted at designated RBridges, which are used to forward multi-destination frames efficiently. Ensuring that multicast replication is configured appropriately and that receivers are reachable through the chosen distribution trees will help avoid unnecessary flooding and maximize the efficiency of TRILL's delivery mechanisms.

In many cases, deploying TRILL involves migrating services from an existing spanning tree domain into the TRILL fabric. This may be done gradually, beginning with the migration of VLANs that are bandwidth-intensive or latency-sensitive, such as those supporting virtualization, storage, or real-time communication systems. During this migration, it is important to verify that end-to-end connectivity is preserved, especially when devices at the edge of the TRILL domain rely on dynamic protocols such as ARP or DHCP. Since TRILL maintains Ethernet semantics, these services generally continue to function without change, but configuration of relay agents and address learning behaviors must be reviewed to ensure compatibility.

Operational visibility becomes increasingly important as TRILL is deployed alongside traditional Ethernet. Monitoring tools must be updated to understand TRILL headers, interpret nickname mappings, and visualize the TRILL topology. Many TRILL-capable devices support extensions to SNMP, streaming telemetry, or proprietary APIs that expose IS-IS topology data, TRILL forwarding tables, and multicast tree information. Leveraging these capabilities provides valuable insight into the network's behavior and helps with troubleshooting, performance optimization, and security monitoring. Integration with existing network management systems ensures continuity in operations while extending control to the newly deployed TRILL segments.

Security considerations are paramount in a hybrid TRILL and legacy environment. Because TRILL introduces a new control plane, protecting it from unauthorized participation is essential. IS-IS authentication must be enabled on all RBridges, and control plane traffic should be isolated from untrusted segments. Edge ports that connect to legacy Ethernet devices should be tightly controlled, with features like port security, dynamic ARP inspection, and MAC limiting enforced to prevent rogue devices from influencing TRILL behavior. Ensuring physical security of RBridges and implementing regular audits of nickname usage and topology changes will further strengthen the deployment's overall security posture.

Deploying TRILL is not only about inserting new devices or enabling new features. It is about shifting the network's operational model from one built on blocked paths and reactive convergence to one built on intelligent path computation and dynamic adaptation. This shift affects how traffic flows, how faults are handled, and how performance is optimized. As the TRILL deployment grows, organizations may choose to expand the TRILL domain deeper into the access layer, eventually replacing legacy switching in those areas as well. The long-term result is a unified Layer 2 fabric that offers the resiliency, scalability, and efficiency traditionally associated with Layer 3 routing, while preserving the simplicity and compatibility of Ethernet.

In summary, deploying TRILL in existing infrastructures offers a flexible and non-disruptive way to modernize network architecture. Through interoperability with legacy protocols, efficient use of redundant links, and a scalable control plane based on IS-IS, TRILL enables organizations to meet growing performance demands while maintaining operational continuity. With careful planning, phased implementation, and strong monitoring and security practices, TRILL can be integrated into existing environments to deliver a more agile, robust, and future-ready network foundation.

TRILL Interoperability and Gateways

The deployment of TRILL, or Transparent Interconnection of Lots of Links, within existing Layer 2 networks presents not only a technological upgrade but also a challenge of seamless interoperability with legacy Ethernet systems and other network domains. Interoperability is a cornerstone of any successful TRILL deployment, ensuring that traffic can flow consistently between TRILL-enabled segments and traditional Ethernet or even Layer 3 domains without service disruption or loss of Ethernet semantics. This is achieved through a combination of protocol design choices, gateway mechanisms, and careful implementation of edge behavior. The goal is to allow TRILL to function as an intelligent, scalable routing layer within a broader Ethernet ecosystem while maintaining full compatibility with non-TRILL devices.

TRILL achieves interoperability primarily through the use of TRILL edge ports, which serve as interfaces between the TRILL domain and traditional Ethernet segments. These ports are responsible for translating between standard Ethernet frames and TRILL-encapsulated frames. When a frame enters the TRILL domain from a legacy device, the edge RBridge encapsulates it with a TRILL header, assigning a destination nickname based on the forwarding database. When the frame reaches its destination RBridge, the TRILL header is removed, and the original Ethernet frame is delivered. This process is transparent to end devices and ensures that TRILL can be introduced without requiring changes to hosts, servers, or network-attached applications.

The key element in TRILL's interoperability strategy is its ability to appear as a single logical bridge to external networks. This is especially important when connecting to devices or segments that use the Spanning Tree Protocol, which operates under the assumption of a loop-free topology enforced through a single spanning tree. Within the TRILL domain, all redundant paths are active and managed through link-state routing and IS-IS, but to the outside, the domain appears as a flat Ethernet segment, preventing any confusion or conflict with spanning tree operations. RBridges automatically recognize whether a connected device is TRILL-capable or not and adjust their behavior accordingly, ensuring that BPDUs from STP-based devices are interpreted and handled without compromising loop prevention.

One of the complexities in TRILL interoperability arises from multicast and broadcast handling. Legacy Ethernet networks use flooding to distribute such traffic, while TRILL uses calculated distribution trees for efficient and loop-free replication. When a multi-destination frame arrives from a legacy segment, the ingress RBridge must determine whether to flood the frame within the TRILL domain and along which distribution tree. It must also avoid sending the frame back into the legacy segment to prevent broadcast storms or loops. This requires a detailed understanding of which ports are considered TRILL core-facing versus legacy-facing and careful configuration of filtering rules to ensure correct frame replication.

In addition to direct interoperability with Ethernet, TRILL networks may also require gateways to connect to Layer 3 networks. These gateways provide the translation between Layer 2 forwarding and Layer 3 routing, acting as interfaces between the TRILL domain and IP-based systems. While TRILL itself does not perform IP routing, it supports integration with standard routing protocols and can coexist with routers that interface with the TRILL domain via access or trunk ports. TRILL-aware gateways must be able to de-encapsulate TRILL frames and forward the payload to the appropriate IP router or routing instance. They also need to maintain awareness of the TRILL topology to ensure optimal forwarding and return path consistency.

In multi-vendor environments, interoperability extends beyond technical translation and into the realm of standards adherence. The TRILL protocol is defined by IETF RFCs, and vendors implementing TRILL are expected to follow these standards to ensure cross-platform compatibility. However, variations in implementation can still occur, particularly in edge behavior, control plane extensions, and management interfaces. Network architects must validate interoperability through testing and certification, especially when deploying RBridges from different manufacturers within the same TRILL domain. Ensuring that all devices support consistent versions of the IS-IS extensions used by TRILL is essential to maintaining a stable control plane.

Gateways also play a crucial role in supporting legacy applications and protocols that may rely on specific Ethernet behaviors. Certain industrial systems, storage technologies, or proprietary network services may expect behavior that differs from TRILL's optimized forwarding. For these scenarios, protocol-aware gateways can provide necessary translation, emulating expected Ethernet characteristics or enforcing special forwarding rules to preserve functionality. These gateways act as intermediaries, adapting TRILL's behavior to meet the expectations of devices or systems that were not designed with link-state Layer 2 routing in mind.

Security is another vital consideration in TRILL interoperability. As TRILL devices interface with legacy systems, they must be protected against spoofing, unauthorized access, and misbehavior originating from non-TRILL segments. This includes implementing MAC filtering, rate limiting, dynamic ARP inspection, and TRILL control plane authentication at gateway points. Legacy devices may not support the same authentication or verification mechanisms as RBridges, so TRILL edge ports and gateways must serve as security boundaries that isolate the core TRILL fabric from potential threats originating at the edge. Furthermore, gateway devices must be monitored for abnormal behavior, and their control plane interactions must be logged and audited regularly to detect anomalies.

Performance considerations also factor into TRILL interoperability and gateway deployment. Translating between TRILL-encapsulated frames and standard Ethernet frames adds processing overhead, which must be accounted for in terms of switch performance and latency. In high-throughput environments, gateway RBridges must be capable of handling large volumes of traffic without bottlenecking the network. This requires careful sizing, appropriate hardware acceleration, and monitoring of buffer utilization and interface queues. Load balancing mechanisms can also be used to distribute gateway responsibilities across multiple RBridges, avoiding single points of failure and improving redundancy.

In scenarios involving virtualization or overlay technologies, TRILL gateways may interface with VXLAN, NVGRE, or other encapsulation formats. These gateways must support multi-encapsulation environments, where TRILL traffic is received on one side and tunneled traffic on the other. This multi-protocol interoperability is essential in modern data centers where TRILL may be used for underlay transport, while overlays provide tenant isolation and segmentation. The gateway must perform appropriate decapsulation and encapsulation operations while maintaining consistent MAC address learning, forwarding policies, and quality of service.

The flexibility of TRILL in adapting to diverse network environments is one of its greatest strengths. By leveraging intelligent gateways and edge functionality, TRILL networks can integrate with legacy systems, bridge to Layer 3 domains, support multicast-aware services, and facilitate application-specific behaviors, all while preserving the efficiency and scalability of link-state Layer 2 routing. A well-implemented TRILL gateway strategy ensures that modernization does not come at the cost of compatibility and that organizations can move forward with next-generation networking without sacrificing the functionality of existing services. Proper planning, adherence to standards, robust monitoring, and strategic deployment of gateways form the foundation for a successful TRILL interoperability model that supports both current needs and future expansion.

Case Studies in TRILL Implementation

Understanding the practical benefits and challenges of deploying TRILL can be greatly enhanced by examining real-world case studies where organizations have implemented TRILL in diverse environments. These implementations demonstrate how TRILL can be tailored to specific network requirements, integrated with legacy systems, and scaled to support complex topologies. They also reveal the design choices, operational strategies, and technical hurdles encountered by network teams seeking to modernize their infrastructure using a Layer 2 routing solution that offers both performance and flexibility.

In one notable case, a large university deployed TRILL to modernize its campus network, which had outgrown the limitations of traditional spanning tree designs. The original architecture consisted of a series of access switches connected to redundant core switches using STP to prevent loops. As new buildings were added and traffic patterns became increasingly unpredictable due to online learning platforms, research data transfers, and real-time collaboration tools, the network began to experience convergence delays and poor link utilization. The university's IT team initiated a phased TRILL deployment starting at the core layer, replacing STP with TRILL-enabled switches that supported IS-IS-based topology discovery and TRILL encapsulation. Over time, they extended TRILL down to the distribution layer, leaving access switches as legacy Ethernet devices connected via TRILL edge ports. The result was a dramatic improvement in convergence time, with failovers occurring in under a second. Load balancing across multiple equal-cost links also allowed for better utilization of available bandwidth. The ability to integrate with existing switches made it possible to maintain network services throughout the migration, allowing the university to upgrade its infrastructure without downtime or disruption.

In a different scenario, a multinational financial services company adopted TRILL in its data center fabric to support rapid growth in virtualized workloads. The company's initial design relied heavily on VLAN-based segmentation across an STP-controlled Layer 2 topology, which created bottlenecks as virtualization density increased. The frequent need to move virtual machines between hypervisors introduced latency and required constant reconfiguration of VLANs, trunk links, and STP priorities. The IT architects chose to implement TRILL across the spine-leaf architecture of the data center, using TRILL-capable spine switches to route traffic intelligently across the fabric. Leaf switches acted as ingress and egress RBridges, encapsulating and decapsulating TRILL frames as needed. This approach allowed for seamless east-west traffic between servers, regardless of their physical location in the data center. The reduced reliance on MAC address flooding and the elimination of blocked links enabled the company to scale its virtual infrastructure with minimal effort. The improved performance of inter-server communication directly translated to faster financial computations and reduced latency in time-sensitive applications such as trading platforms and risk modeling engines.

Another compelling implementation occurred in a media production company that required a low-latency, high-throughput network to support video editing and rendering workflows distributed across multiple facilities. The company faced issues with STP-related link blocking and limited bandwidth availability during peak production hours. Their engineers opted to create a TRILL backbone that connected various server farms and editing suites using high-speed fiber links. Each facility maintained its own access layer running legacy Ethernet, but traffic between sites was routed using TRILL. By assigning nicknames to each RBridge and using TRILL's IS-IS control plane to compute optimal paths, the network was able to dynamically route large video files between locations without congestion. The implementation of ECMP in the TRILL fabric allowed parallel file transfers across multiple paths, significantly reducing delivery times for rendered content. Additionally, the team implemented multicast distribution trees to support real-time streaming of live editing sessions. The reliability and performance improvements provided by TRILL enabled the company to operate a highly collaborative and distributed content production model without sacrificing quality or consistency.

A fourth case involved a government agency responsible for managing a secure and isolated network for classified communications. The agency's network design emphasized strict segmentation and minimal exposure to external devices, which made conventional routing protocols unsuitable due to their reliance on IP addresses and global reachability. The engineers selected TRILL because of its MAC-based forwarding, compatibility with existing security appliances, and built-in loop prevention without the need for spanning tree. The TRILL deployment was limited to an enclosed environment, with a fixed set of RBridges participating in a private control plane using authenticated IS-IS sessions. Each RBridge was configured with manually assigned nicknames and MAC filters to enforce traffic policies. The ability to build redundant paths and fast-failover mechanisms using TRILL proved invaluable during simulated attack scenarios, where rapid reconvergence and containment of affected segments were critical. The network's ability to maintain Layer 2 services while enforcing strict traffic isolation made it an ideal fit for sensitive workloads that demanded both operational continuity and security assurance.

An additional case involved a regional healthcare provider that needed to consolidate its network infrastructure after acquiring several clinics and specialty centers. Each site had previously operated as a standalone network, with its own VLANs and spanning tree configuration. The central IT department sought to create a unified network that could connect all locations while simplifying management and enabling centralized access to electronic health records, imaging data, and communications systems. They designed a TRILL-based wide area backbone that connected each clinic via TRILL edge gateways, allowing each local network to retain its existing Layer 2 configuration while seamlessly routing inter-site traffic through TRILL. The backbone provided redundancy and rapid convergence in case of link failure, ensuring that critical medical services remained online even during maintenance or outages. The scalability of TRILL also allowed the IT team to add new clinics with minimal changes, as each new location simply required the configuration of an edge RBridge and its integration into the TRILL topology. This approach gave the healthcare provider the performance of a routed core while preserving the flexibility and simplicity of Ethernet for day-to-day operations.

These case studies reveal that TRILL can be successfully adapted to a variety of environments, each with unique goals and constraints. Whether enhancing campus connectivity, optimizing data center performance, supporting multimedia production, enabling secure communications, or unifying dispersed networks, TRILL provides a robust framework that combines the best features of Ethernet and routing. Its ability to interoperate with existing infrastructure, support gradual deployment, and deliver intelligent path selection and fast failover makes it a powerful tool for organizations facing the challenges of modern networking. Each deployment serves as a blueprint for what is possible when TRILL is used strategically, reinforcing its value as a transformative solution for scalable and resilient Layer 2 networking.

Future Directions Beyond TRILL

The development and adoption of TRILL, or Transparent Interconnection of Lots of Links, marked a pivotal evolution in Layer 2 networking. TRILL successfully addressed many of the long-standing limitations of traditional Ethernet, particularly in relation to scalability, path optimization, and convergence speed. It introduced link-state routing concepts into Ethernet switching, enabled multipathing, and offered a more intelligent control plane through IS-IS. However, as data center architectures, virtualization technologies, and cloud-native applications have continued to evolve at a rapid pace, new challenges and expectations have emerged that require more than what TRILL was originally designed to provide. This ongoing transformation in the networking landscape has led to the exploration of technologies and paradigms that go beyond TRILL, each aiming to provide greater flexibility, programmability, and performance in environments where agility and scalability are paramount.

One of the most significant shifts beyond TRILL has been the move toward overlay network technologies. Protocols such as VXLAN, NVGRE, and GENEVE have gained widespread adoption, particularly in large-scale cloud data centers and service provider networks. These overlay protocols encapsulate Layer 2 frames within IP packets, allowing networks to be built over Layer 3 infrastructures. This encapsulation approach offers enhanced scalability by leveraging the proven stability and reach of IP routing, while still supporting the Layer 2 semantics that many applications and virtual machines rely on. In contrast to TRILL, which is fundamentally a Layer 2 routing protocol, overlay networks allow for decoupled underlays and overlays, enabling better multi-tenancy, segmentation, and mobility. The flexibility of VXLAN, in particular, has made it the de facto standard for software-defined data center networking, enabling virtual networks to span across geographic boundaries without relying on physical Layer 2 connectivity.

The rise of Software-Defined Networking has further altered the trajectory of network design, shifting control away from distributed protocols like TRILL and toward centralized controllers. SDN frameworks allow for the separation of the control and data planes, enabling administrators to program the behavior of the entire network through APIs and automation tools. In SDN environments, the role of protocols like TRILL becomes diminished as path computation, policy enforcement, and traffic engineering are handled by centralized software entities. SDN platforms can simulate or replace many of the features that TRILL provides, such as multipathing and fast failover, but with greater visibility and dynamic control. This shift allows networks to adapt in real time to workload demands, security events, and application-level requirements. Technologies like OpenFlow and intent-based networking further this paradigm by giving operators the ability to define desired outcomes rather than configuring individual devices.

Another direction being explored beyond TRILL is the adoption of routing in the data center fabric itself. Technologies such as EVPN (Ethernet VPN) over VXLAN have gained traction as a comprehensive solution for both Layer 2 and Layer 3 connectivity in multi-tenant environments. EVPN provides control-plane signaling using BGP, allowing for MAC address learning to occur via routes rather than flooding. This model reduces broadcast traffic, enhances security, and improves convergence. EVPN-VXLAN has effectively become a successor to TRILL in many modern architectures, combining the benefits of overlay networks with mature and scalable routing protocols. It also aligns more closely with the operational models of service providers, who are already familiar with BGP as a cornerstone protocol.

Meanwhile, the concept of intent-based networking continues to reshape expectations around network automation and intelligence. Rather than focusing on protocols and configurations, intent-based systems interpret high-level business or application objectives and automatically translate them into network policies and behaviors. In such environments, the complexity of traditional protocols is abstracted away, and their role is reduced to simply executing the instructions derived from the intent. This means that protocols like TRILL may no longer need to play an active role in path selection or topology management, as those decisions are dynamically orchestrated by AI-driven or logic-based controllers. This vision points to a future where the network becomes a responsive service platform, able to self-configure, self-optimize, and self-heal without human intervention.

The need for microsegmentation and granular security controls has also influenced the movement beyond TRILL. While TRILL provides a secure control plane and avoids many of the vulnerabilities associated with STP, it lacks the fine-grained segmentation features required in zero-trust architectures. Modern environments require isolation down to the workload level, often enforced through policies that are independent of IP addressing or VLAN structure. Network function virtualization and service chaining have become critical components in enforcing these policies, and they often rely on overlay networks and SDN to direct traffic through inspection points and policy engines. TRILL, with its MAC-based forwarding and flat topology assumptions, is less equipped to meet these advanced security requirements.

As containerization and Kubernetes-based orchestration have become dominant in application deployment, the network must support highly dynamic and ephemeral workloads. Traditional protocols, even advanced ones like TRILL, were not designed to handle the constant churn of IP and MAC address allocations that occurs in such environments. Container networking solutions often rely on custom overlays, CNI plugins, and Kubernetes-native networking models that provide rapid service discovery, load balancing, and namespace isolation. These platforms expect the network to be programmable and responsive, qualities that align more closely with SDN and overlay-based models than with traditional distributed control protocols.

Hardware evolution has also played a role in redefining the network beyond TRILL. With the rise of programmable network devices, such as those using P4 or other data-plane programming languages, network behavior can now be customized at the silicon level. This allows for the implementation of entirely new forwarding paradigms, telemetry functions, and security models that go far beyond the capabilities of fixed-protocol devices. These programmable switches and NICs enable in-network processing, real-time visibility, and ultra-low latency forwarding tailored to specific workloads or application flows.

Despite the shift toward newer technologies, the legacy of TRILL remains relevant. It helped transition the industry away from blocked paths and tree-based topologies and introduced a distributed routing mentality at Layer 2 that paved the way for more modern designs. The lessons learned from TRILL's implementation—such as the value of fast convergence, loop-free multipath forwarding, and MAC address abstraction—continue to influence how networks are built and managed. As organizations evaluate the future of their networks, TRILL serves as a milestone on the journey toward more intelligent, agile, and automated infrastructures, even as the spotlight shifts to overlays, SDN, and intent-based models.

In the years ahead, the networking industry will likely continue its evolution toward abstraction, programmability, and policy-driven design. Technologies beyond TRILL will focus increasingly on delivering end-to-end service assurance, application-awareness, and seamless multi-cloud connectivity. While TRILL may no longer be at the forefront of innovation, its impact will persist in the foundations it helped establish and in the design principles it inspired. Understanding TRILL's role in the broader context of networking evolution is essential for any architect or engineer seeking to design networks that are ready for the challenges of tomorrow.

Understanding Ethernet Fabric Technologies

Ethernet fabric technologies represent a transformative shift in how data centers and enterprise networks are architected, offering a more intelligent, scalable, and resilient approach to Layer 2 connectivity. These technologies extend the traditional Ethernet model by introducing mechanisms that enable greater network automation, loop-free topologies, consistent configurations, and optimized traffic paths. Unlike legacy Ethernet, which depends on spanning tree protocols to avoid loops by disabling redundant links, Ethernet fabrics use distributed control planes or centralized management to ensure every link remains active and available. This results in better bandwidth utilization, faster convergence, and improved network agility, all of which are essential in environments driven by virtualization, cloud computing, and dynamic application workloads.

At the heart of Ethernet fabric technology is the idea of flattening the network topology. In traditional hierarchical designs, traffic flows are forced through multiple layers of switches—access, distribution, and core—resulting in bottlenecks, complexity, and suboptimal paths. Ethernet fabrics aim to collapse these layers into a more mesh-like structure where every switch can participate equally in the forwarding process. This design reduces latency, simplifies configuration, and supports the east-west traffic patterns that dominate modern data centers. With Ethernet fabric, devices communicate through the shortest available path rather than being confined by the rigid hierarchy imposed by spanning tree.

One of the key enablers of Ethernet fabric technology is the use of control protocols that distribute forwarding information across all switches in the fabric. These protocols may include TRILL, Shortest Path Bridging (SPB), or vendor-specific implementations such as Cisco FabricPath or Brocade VCS. Each switch in the fabric becomes aware of the overall topology and can independently compute the best path to a given destination. This awareness eliminates the need for flooding and learning at every node, reducing control-plane overhead and accelerating convergence. With a complete view of the network, switches can make forwarding decisions based on the most current state of the fabric, ensuring fast recovery from link or node failures and consistent traffic engineering.

Ethernet fabrics also support the concept of multipathing at Layer 2, allowing multiple equal-cost paths between any two nodes to be used simultaneously. This is in contrast to legacy Ethernet, where spanning tree blocks all but one path between nodes to prevent loops. In a fabric environment, all available paths are used, resulting in improved throughput, fault tolerance, and load balancing. This feature is particularly important in dense environments such as virtualized data centers, where traffic volumes are high and link utilization must be maximized to maintain performance. By using hashing algorithms to distribute traffic across multiple links, Ethernet fabrics can ensure efficient use of resources and avoid congestion on any single path.

Another important aspect of Ethernet fabric technologies is the simplification of configuration and management. Traditional Ethernet networks often require per-device configuration, which can lead to inconsistencies and human error. In a fabric, configuration is abstracted and propagated automatically across the infrastructure. When a new switch is added to the fabric, it learns the topology and inherits the appropriate policies and configurations without manual intervention. This plug-and-play behavior accelerates deployment and minimizes operational overhead. It also aligns well with modern IT practices such as DevOps and infrastructure as code, where automation and repeatability are crucial.

Ethernet fabrics are also designed to support virtualization and cloud services at scale. They provide the foundation for virtual machine mobility by preserving MAC and VLAN information across the fabric, ensuring that virtual machines can move seamlessly between physical hosts without the need for reconfiguration or topology recalculation. This capability is essential in environments that use live migration technologies, such as VMware vMotion or Hyper-V Live Migration, where virtual machines must maintain network connectivity and consistent performance during transitions. By extending Layer 2 connectivity across the entire fabric without compromising loop prevention or performance, Ethernet fabrics enable more agile and responsive data center operations.

Security is another area where Ethernet fabric technologies offer advantages. By centralizing control and using authenticated protocols, fabrics reduce the risk of topology manipulation or unauthorized access. Some implementations support policy-based access control, where security rules are enforced based on user identity, device type, or application, rather than relying solely on IP addresses or VLAN segmentation. This granular control allows organizations to implement microsegmentation, limiting the attack surface and improving containment in the event of a breach. The consistency of fabric-based security policies also simplifies compliance and auditing, making it easier to enforce regulatory requirements and internal standards.

In multi-tenant environments, such as colocation data centers or service provider networks, Ethernet fabrics enable the segmentation of tenants without the complexity of VLAN sprawl or manual provisioning. Each tenant can be assigned its own virtual network within the fabric, isolated from other tenants while still sharing the same physical infrastructure. This model supports scalability and operational efficiency, as new tenants can be onboarded quickly and securely. The underlying fabric ensures that tenant traffic remains isolated and follows the most efficient path through the network, regardless of physical location or topological constraints.

Ethernet fabrics also pave the way for integration with higher-layer network services and automation platforms. They provide the consistent, reliable foundation needed for orchestration tools to deploy applications, enforce policies, and monitor performance. By exposing telemetry and programmable interfaces, fabric-enabled switches can report real-time metrics, alert on anomalies, and adapt to changing workloads. This visibility and control are essential in modern IT environments where applications must scale dynamically, respond to demand, and recover from failures without manual intervention.

The continued evolution of Ethernet fabric technologies reflects the broader trend toward more intelligent and adaptable networks. As data volumes grow, workloads become more dynamic, and user expectations increase, traditional Ethernet approaches are no longer sufficient. Ethernet fabrics represent the next step in meeting these demands, offering a network model that is inherently scalable, efficient, and resilient. Whether deployed in enterprise data centers, cloud infrastructures, or service provider networks, Ethernet fabrics are becoming the new standard for building high-performance Layer 2 environments that can meet the complex requirements of today's digital landscape. Understanding how these fabrics operate, what they enable, and how they integrate with broader network strategies is essential for any organization seeking to modernize its infrastructure and prepare for future growth.

VXLAN and Overlay Alternatives to STP

The evolution of modern data centers and enterprise networks has introduced demands that legacy protocols like the Spanning Tree Protocol can no longer efficiently satisfy. While STP was groundbreaking in its ability to prevent loops in Layer 2 Ethernet topologies, its limitations in terms of scalability, convergence speed, and path utilization have become increasingly apparent in virtualized and cloud-native environments. Technologies such as VXLAN, or Virtual Extensible LAN, have emerged as powerful alternatives, enabling the creation of overlay networks that abstract Layer 2 segments over Layer 3 infrastructures. These overlays not only bypass the limitations of STP but also introduce enhanced flexibility, segmentation, and scalability that align with the needs of contemporary network architectures.

VXLAN operates by encapsulating Layer 2 Ethernet frames within UDP packets, allowing them to be transmitted across Layer 3 networks. This encapsulation extends the reach of Layer 2 domains without requiring physical adjacency or STP-based loop prevention. Instead of relying on a single active path as enforced by STP, VXLAN supports multipath forwarding using the Equal Cost Multipath capabilities of modern IP routing. This change allows for far better utilization of available bandwidth and introduces redundancy without the constraints of blocked links. In a VXLAN-based network, traffic can be dynamically balanced across several links, significantly enhancing throughput and reducing the risk of congestion.

A key enabler of VXLAN is the concept of the VTEP, or VXLAN Tunnel Endpoint. VTEPs are responsible for encapsulating and decapsulating VXLAN packets at the edge of the overlay. Each VTEP maintains a mapping table that associates virtual network identifiers with destination IP addresses of remote VTEPs. These mappings may be learned through various control plane mechanisms or configured statically. The most scalable and efficient implementations rely on control plane protocols like BGP EVPN, which allow VXLAN overlays to use BGP to distribute MAC address and VTEP mappings. This separation of the control plane from the data plane reduces broadcast and flooding and allows for fast convergence in the event of topology changes.

One of the most important features of VXLAN is the VXLAN Network Identifier, or VNI. This 24-bit field in the VXLAN header allows for the creation of up to sixteen million unique Layer 2 segments, far exceeding the 4096 VLAN limit imposed by IEEE 802.1Q. This abundance of virtual segments makes VXLAN particularly well suited for multi-tenant environments and large-scale data centers, where tenant isolation and fine-grained segmentation are essential. Each tenant can be assigned its own VNI, creating a logically isolated network that can span across multiple physical locations without interference from other tenants or segments.

Overlay technologies like VXLAN also facilitate better support for modern application deployment models. In environments with high levels of virtualization and containerization, applications are frequently moved, scaled, or instantiated across different hosts. Traditional Layer 2 networks struggle to maintain consistent connectivity during these operations, often requiring manual reconfiguration or complex workarounds. VXLAN overlays abstract the physical network, enabling seamless mobility of workloads while preserving IP and MAC address consistency. When paired with orchestration platforms like OpenStack or Kubernetes, VXLAN provides the underlying network fabric that enables on-demand provisioning and automated scaling of services.

Another major advantage of VXLAN over STP is its compatibility with existing IP routing infrastructure. Since VXLAN tunnels are transmitted over IP, they can traverse any Layer 3 network, leveraging existing routing protocols and topologies. This compatibility reduces the need for special-purpose hardware and simplifies the integration of VXLAN into brownfield environments. Organizations can incrementally adopt VXLAN by deploying VTEPs at key locations and connecting them over the existing routed backbone. This approach avoids the need for large-scale network redesigns and minimizes service disruption during migration.

The elimination of Layer 2 flooding is another area where VXLAN dramatically improves upon STP-based designs. In traditional Ethernet, unknown unicast, broadcast, and multicast frames must be flooded to all ports in a VLAN. This behavior consumes bandwidth and increases the processing burden on switches. VXLAN, particularly when paired with BGP EVPN, replaces flooding with controlled distribution. MAC address reachability is advertised through BGP, allowing VTEPs to make precise forwarding decisions without flooding the network. Broadcast and multicast traffic can be replicated only where necessary or completely avoided using head-end replication and selective forwarding mechanisms.

VXLAN also integrates well with security and policy enforcement technologies. Overlay networks can be augmented with security group policies, firewalls, and microsegmentation engines that operate independently of the physical network. Because the overlay abstracts the underlying infrastructure, security policies can follow workloads as they move across the data center, ensuring consistent protection regardless of their physical location. This capability is essential in zero trust environments, where access controls and inspection must be enforced dynamically and pervasively. With overlays, security is no longer tied to VLAN boundaries or port-based configurations, but instead can be defined based on identity, role, or application context.

Performance is another area where VXLAN delivers advantages. Unlike STP, which blocks links to prevent loops, VXLAN actively utilizes all available paths. This means that spine-leaf topologies and Clos fabrics can be fully leveraged, delivering high throughput and low latency. The use of hardware offloading for VXLAN encapsulation and decapsulation in modern network interface cards and switches further enhances performance, allowing VXLAN to be deployed at scale without introducing significant overhead. Hardware acceleration ensures that encapsulated traffic is processed at line rate, maintaining the performance characteristics required for latency-sensitive applications and large-scale data workloads.

As networks continue to evolve toward greater automation, programmability, and responsiveness, overlay technologies like VXLAN provide the flexibility and scalability that are essential for next-generation architectures. They decouple the logical topology from the physical infrastructure, enabling networks to adapt to application needs rather than forcing applications to conform to network constraints. This shift empowers IT teams to deliver services faster, respond to changes more effectively, and ensure consistent policy enforcement across complex and distributed environments.

VXLAN represents a significant advancement over STP by providing a more scalable, resilient, and efficient foundation for modern networking. It overcomes the limitations of legacy Ethernet by introducing overlay principles, supporting massive segmentation, enabling multipath forwarding, and integrating with existing IP infrastructures. When combined with control plane protocols like EVPN, it delivers a powerful framework for building automated, high-performance, and secure networks. As organizations embrace digital transformation, virtualization, and cloud-native technologies, VXLAN and similar overlay solutions offer the tools needed to meet the demands of today's connected world while laying the groundwork for the future of network design.

Data Center Bridging and STP Coexistence

In the evolving landscape of enterprise computing, data centers have become the backbone of digital operations, supporting a diverse range of services from cloud computing to storage virtualization and real-time application hosting. Traditional Ethernet, while effective in many networking scenarios, was never designed to handle the unique demands of data center environments, particularly in relation to loss-sensitive storage traffic, low-latency applications, and high levels of east-west communication. To address these challenges, the IEEE developed a suite of enhancements under the umbrella of Data Center

Bridging, or DCB, which introduces critical improvements to conventional Ethernet while still enabling backward compatibility with existing protocols, including the Spanning Tree Protocol. Understanding how DCB functions and coexists with STP is essential for network engineers aiming to modernize data center infrastructure without causing disruption to legacy systems.

Data Center Bridging is not a single protocol but rather a collection of extensions to Ethernet standards. These enhancements include Priority-based Flow Control, Enhanced Transmission Selection, Congestion Notification, and Data Center Bridging Exchange protocol. Together, they enable Ethernet to behave more like a lossless transport medium, which is particularly beneficial for storage protocols such as Fibre Channel over Ethernet. In traditional Ethernet, packet loss due to congestion is expected and managed through retransmissions at higher layers. However, storage traffic cannot tolerate loss in the same way, and the performance implications of dropped frames are severe. Priority-based Flow Control, or PFC, addresses this issue by allowing selective pausing of traffic based on priority levels, ensuring that critical flows such as storage can continue without interruption even during periods of congestion.

Enhanced Transmission Selection complements PFC by providing bandwidth management across different traffic classes. It ensures that high-priority traffic receives guaranteed minimum bandwidth while allowing fair sharing of excess bandwidth among other classes. This is especially important in mixed workloads, where storage, video, and general-purpose traffic may all be traversing the same physical infrastructure. By enforcing traffic isolation and ensuring consistent performance across all applications, DCB facilitates more predictable and manageable data center behavior. Congestion Notification further enhances this capability by enabling end-to-end congestion awareness. When a switch detects congestion, it can notify upstream devices, prompting them to slow down transmission rates before packet loss occurs. This proactive mechanism reduces the likelihood of queue overflows and maintains stability in high-throughput environments.

While DCB brings these advanced features to Ethernet, it does not inherently replace the role of the Spanning Tree Protocol in loop prevention. Many legacy switches and edge devices within a data center still rely on STP to manage Layer 2 loops and ensure network stability. In environments where DCB is deployed, but older equipment remains in use, both systems must coexist without introducing operational conflicts. This coexistence requires careful configuration and adherence to design best practices that account for the differences in behavior between traditional STP domains and DCB-enhanced networks. Typically, DCB is implemented within specific segments of the data center where its benefits are most needed, such as between top-of-rack switches and storage arrays. STP may still operate on uplinks to aggregation or core layers, particularly when those layers include legacy infrastructure or are shared with broader enterprise networks.

One strategy to enable seamless coexistence is to logically isolate the DCB domain from the STP domain. This can be achieved through VLAN segmentation or the use of separate virtual interfaces. By creating clear boundaries, traffic within the DCB zone benefits from advanced flow control and congestion management, while STP remains active on external interfaces to maintain loop prevention. In this hybrid model, care must be taken to prevent unintended interactions. For instance, PFC should not be enabled on ports that participate in STP, as the pause frames used by PFC can disrupt BPDUs and interfere with spanning tree operations. Likewise, STP should be configured to ignore BPDUs on interfaces where DCB protocols are active to avoid false topology changes or misinterpretation of control messages.

Another consideration is the impact of link failures and convergence times. While STP relies on timers and port state transitions to detect and respond to topology changes, DCB assumes that links remain stable and relies on rapid reaction to congestion and flow control events. In mixed environments, link failures can lead to inconsistent behavior unless convergence mechanisms are aligned. Implementing Rapid Spanning Tree Protocol on STP-enabled segments can help narrow the gap in convergence times and provide a more harmonious interaction with DCB domains. Some modern switches support dynamic adjustment of PFC and DCB parameters based on link state, allowing for adaptive behavior when topology changes are detected.

Monitoring and management tools also play a critical role in maintaining coexistence. Network visibility must span both DCB and STP domains to provide a comprehensive understanding of performance, congestion, and fault conditions. Metrics such as PFC pause frames, queue lengths, STP topology changes, and congestion notification messages should be tracked and correlated to identify issues early. Most DCB-capable devices expose these metrics through standard interfaces such as SNMP or streaming telemetry, making them accessible to existing network monitoring platforms. Configuration management tools can also enforce policy consistency across hybrid domains, ensuring that critical settings are preserved during software updates or device replacements.

Security is another aspect that must be considered when deploying DCB alongside STP. The presence of legacy devices introduces vulnerabilities that DCB alone cannot mitigate. For example, STP remains susceptible to BPDU spoofing and root bridge manipulation, especially if edge ports are not properly secured. While DCB brings improvements in traffic handling, it does not include inherent authentication or encryption. It is therefore essential to enforce traditional security measures, including port security, MAC address filtering, and control-plane policing, particularly at the points where DCB and STP domains intersect. Combining these controls with DCB's enhanced traffic management creates a more robust and resilient network posture.

As data centers continue to evolve, the need to integrate new technologies with legacy systems will remain a constant challenge. Data Center Bridging offers a powerful set of tools for improving Ethernet performance in critical areas like storage and virtualization, but its full potential is only realized when it is carefully integrated into the broader network environment. Coexistence with STP is not only possible but necessary in many transitional architectures. With thoughtful design, clear segmentation, and comprehensive monitoring, organizations can leverage the benefits of both technologies, creating a hybrid network that supports current operational needs while laying the groundwork for future innovation. Understanding how DCB and STP interact, where their boundaries lie, and how they influence each other is crucial to building a data center fabric that is both high-performing and resilient.

Hybrid Networks Using TRILL and MSTP

The process of modernizing a network is often gradual and complex, requiring the integration of new technologies with legacy protocols that continue to serve critical parts of the infrastructure. One of the more nuanced deployments in contemporary enterprise and data center environments involves the coexistence of TRILL, or Transparent Interconnection of Lots of Links, with Multiple Spanning Tree Protocol, or MSTP. These two technologies represent different generations of Layer 2 control mechanisms. TRILL introduces link-state routing at Layer 2 to overcome the inefficiencies of blocking links and slow convergence in legacy spanning tree designs, while MSTP offers VLAN-aware loop prevention and logical segmentation through instance mapping. In many organizations, replacing all devices with TRILL-capable hardware is not immediately feasible, making it essential to understand how to implement and operate hybrid networks that incorporate both TRILL and MSTP elements.

Deploying TRILL in an existing MSTP network typically starts with the strategic insertion of TRILL-capable devices, called RBridges, into the core or aggregation layers of the network where path optimization, convergence speed, and loop-free multipathing offer the greatest benefits. These RBridges form the TRILL domain and operate using the IS-IS link-state routing protocol to exchange topology information and calculate shortest path forwarding trees. Surrounding this domain, access switches and other segments may continue to run MSTP, supporting VLAN-based segmentation and blocking redundant links to prevent loops in areas that do not yet benefit from TRILL's advanced capabilities. The boundary between these two domains becomes critical, requiring careful configuration to ensure that loop prevention is maintained and that traffic flows correctly between the MSTP and TRILL environments.

The primary interface between TRILL and MSTP segments is the TRILL edge port, which connects the RBridge to non-TRILL devices. These edge ports are capable of forwarding standard Ethernet frames and handling the translation between encapsulated TRILL traffic and conventional Layer 2 Ethernet. When a frame enters the TRILL domain from an MSTP segment, the ingress RBridge encapsulates it with a TRILL header, indicating the egress RBridge responsible for delivering the frame to its final destination. At the other end, the egress RBridge decapsulates the frame and forwards it using standard Ethernet mechanisms. From the perspective of the MSTP domain, the TRILL fabric functions as a single virtual bridge that appears to participate in the spanning tree topology, maintaining compatibility with MSTP's BPDU-based loop prevention logic.

In such a hybrid network, the coordination of topology management is essential. MSTP determines the root bridge and blocks or forwards ports based on VLAN-instance associations, while TRILL relies on IS-IS link-state advertisements and Dijkstra's algorithm to compute forwarding paths across the entire TRILL domain. Since MSTP uses a reactive and timer-driven process to recalculate topologies, it is generally slower to respond to changes compared to TRILL's event-driven convergence. To avoid instability, it is important that MSTP does not attempt to interpret or override the internal behavior of the TRILL fabric. This is achieved by configuring the TRILL domain to suppress or filter BPDUs at edge ports, effectively isolating the TRILL control plane from MSTP's influence. At the same time, MSTP edge switches should treat their TRILL-connected uplinks as connections to a single logical bridge, reducing the risk of misinterpreting multiple RBridge paths as topology loops.

Another challenge in hybrid networks involves the handling of VLANs across both domains. MSTP uses VLAN-to-instance mapping to manage different Layer 2 topologies for different groups of VLANs, allowing for more granular load balancing and failover behaviors. TRILL, in contrast, treats each VLAN as a separate instance and calculates a unique distribution tree for multi-destination traffic within that VLAN. When bridging VLANs between MSTP and TRILL, the RBridge must preserve VLAN tagging while ensuring consistent forwarding behavior. Careful mapping of VLANs and alignment of VLAN IDs across both domains is necessary to avoid traffic loops, VLAN leaks, or duplicate frames. Any inconsistencies in VLAN configurations can lead to broadcast storms or unpredictable path selection, especially in environments where multiple MSTP instances share redundant links with the TRILL domain.

To support hybrid operation, network administrators must also ensure that MAC address learning remains consistent across the network. In TRILL, MAC addresses are associated with RBridge nicknames and learned through encapsulated traffic that identifies ingress and egress points. In MSTP, MAC learning is based on traditional flooding and frame arrival interfaces. When a host in the MSTP domain communicates with a host in the TRILL domain, the RBridge must correctly associate the host's MAC address with the appropriate egress nickname and distribute that information throughout the TRILL domain. Conversely, when traffic returns from TRILL to MSTP, the egress RBridge must deliver the frame through the correct edge port so that it reaches the intended recipient in the legacy segment.

Operational visibility and diagnostics are also more complex in hybrid environments. MSTP provides basic logging and topology change notifications, while TRILL includes IS-IS link-state information, nickname mappings, and encapsulation data. Monitoring tools must collect and correlate information from both control planes to provide a unified view of the network. Troubleshooting tools should support the ability to trace a frame from a host in the MSTP domain through the TRILL fabric and back again, identifying potential misconfigurations or path inconsistencies. Events such as topology changes, link failures, or load balancing shifts must be interpreted in the context of both protocols, especially if traffic traverses multiple domains with different convergence behaviors and failure responses.

Security is another critical consideration in hybrid networks. While MSTP is vulnerable to BPDU spoofing and root bridge attacks, TRILL's use of IS-IS and link-state logic makes it more resistant to such manipulation. At the same time, any unprotected edge port in the MSTP domain could become an entry point for malicious activity if it is not properly secured. All edge ports connecting MSTP to TRILL should implement port security, BPDU filtering, and MAC limiting to reduce the attack surface. Where possible, authentication should be applied to the IS-IS control plane within the TRILL domain to ensure that only authorized RBridges participate in topology advertisements and path calculations.

Despite the complexity of hybrid TRILL and MSTP networks, they provide a realistic pathway for organizations seeking to modernize their networks without committing to a full replacement of existing infrastructure. By allowing both technologies to operate side by side, organizations can incrementally upgrade performance-critical segments to TRILL while continuing to leverage the stability and familiarity of MSTP in less dynamic areas. This dual approach balances innovation with operational continuity, supporting modern applications and traffic patterns while respecting budgetary constraints and technical risk. A well-designed hybrid network combines the strengths of both TRILL and MSTP, ensuring resilience, scalability, and adaptability in an increasingly complex networking landscape.

Monitoring and Troubleshooting STP

The Spanning Tree Protocol is a foundational component of traditional Layer 2 Ethernet networks, designed to prevent loops by creating a loop-free logical topology among interconnected switches. Despite its widespread use and effectiveness, STP can become a source of significant network instability if not monitored and managed properly. Understanding how to observe the behavior of STP, interpret its output, and troubleshoot problems is essential for any network professional responsible for maintaining reliable and high-performing Ethernet infrastructures. When issues related to STP arise, they often impact large portions of the network and can be difficult to isolate due to the distributed nature of the protocol and the lack of immediate visibility into its internal processes without proper tools and techniques.

Monitoring STP begins with an awareness of its basic operation. STP uses Bridge Protocol Data Units to share information among switches about bridge IDs, root bridge elections, and port roles. These BPDUs are exchanged at regular intervals and are critical for maintaining the current topology. Any interruption in BPDU exchange, such as a dropped BPDU or a misconfiguration that filters BPDUs, can result in a topology recalculation, causing certain ports to transition between blocking and forwarding states. During this recalculation period, traffic may be disrupted, and broadcast storms or loops may occur if STP does not converge quickly or if the network design introduces ambiguity in path selection.

Network operators can begin monitoring STP by examining the root bridge selection process. The root bridge is the focal point of the STP topology, and all path calculations are made in relation to it. Each switch determines its path to the root bridge and assigns port roles such as root port, designated port, or blocked port based on the path cost. Regularly verifying which switch has assumed the root bridge role is crucial, as an unintended device becoming root can alter traffic paths and introduce performance degradation. Monitoring tools should alert administrators when the root bridge changes, especially if the new root has a higher bridge priority or resides in an unexpected segment of the network.

To gather information about STP, network engineers should use built-in commands available on most managed switches. These commands display information such as the current root bridge, the bridge ID of the local switch, the status of each port, timers, and the state of STP instances across different VLANs. For networks running Rapid Spanning Tree Protocol or Multiple Spanning Tree Protocol, additional output may include instance-specific roles and mappings. This information allows engineers to verify that the topology aligns with the intended design and helps identify potential misconfigurations such as inconsistent bridge priorities or incorrect port cost assignments.

Log files and event messages also play a vital role in monitoring STP activity. Many switches generate log entries when a topology change occurs, when BPDUs are lost, or when ports transition between STP states. These logs can be centralized using a syslog server and analyzed for patterns, such as frequent topology changes in a specific VLAN, which may indicate flapping links, duplex mismatches, or a faulty switch. STP topology change notifications also affect MAC address learning, as entries in the MAC address table may be flushed prematurely, leading to increased flooding and degraded performance. By correlating topology change logs with MAC table behavior, engineers can pinpoint the root cause of intermittent connectivity or unexplained packet loss.

Troubleshooting STP requires a methodical approach. The first step is to verify the expected root bridge and confirm that it matches the intended design. If an unexpected switch has become root, engineers should inspect its bridge priority settings and make adjustments as necessary. In most networks, the root bridge should be a stable and centrally located switch with high capacity and redundancy. Once the root bridge is verified, the next step is to examine port roles and verify that root ports and designated ports are assigned correctly. Inconsistent port roles across neighboring switches often indicate a mismatch in link cost or a failure to receive BPDUs.

Another common issue involves ports that remain in a blocking state longer than necessary. This can be caused by excessive STP timers or improper link detection mechanisms. Engineers should ensure that portfast or edge-port configurations are used on access ports connected to end devices, which prevents these ports from entering the blocking state and speeds up convergence. In networks running RSTP, rapid transition to forwarding can be enabled through edge-type and point-to-point link detection. However, improper configuration of these features may cause loops if applied to inter-switch links. Careful documentation and validation of port roles and link types are essential in preventing misbehavior.

One of the most challenging aspects of STP troubleshooting is identifying transient loops. These loops may occur during topology recalculation or as a result of flapping links that cause rapid state changes. In such cases, broadcast or multicast traffic may flood the network, consuming bandwidth and overwhelming switches. Tools such as packet captures, loop detection features, and interface statistics can help isolate these loops. Engineers should look for ports experiencing high levels of inbound broadcast traffic or unusual CPU utilization on switches, which may indicate control-plane saturation caused by a loop or topology instability.

Physical layer issues can also manifest as STP problems. A faulty cable, bad transceiver, or intermittent power to a switch can cause link flapping, which in turn triggers frequent topology recalculations. These events may not be immediately attributed to STP, making it essential to correlate STP events with physical interface logs. Using features like link-state tracking, event correlation, and interface reliability counters helps distinguish between protocol issues and hardware failures.

Advanced troubleshooting may also involve simulating STP topologies or using virtual labs to replicate problematic configurations. By recreating the STP environment in a controlled setting, engineers can test different scenarios, analyze BPDU behavior, and verify how the network reacts to changes in configuration or topology. This practice improves the team's readiness to address live incidents and helps in building more robust designs that prevent similar issues in the future.

Maintaining visibility into STP behavior is not a one-time task but an ongoing process. Networks change over time, new devices are added, and old links are repurposed. Each of these changes can introduce new variables into the STP topology, potentially undermining previous assumptions about stability and convergence. Periodic audits of the STP configuration, combined with continuous monitoring and timely response to alerts, help ensure that STP remains an asset rather than a liability in the network. For critical networks, incorporating STP-aware monitoring platforms and ensuring that the entire engineering team is familiar with interpreting STP metrics are key to maintaining uninterrupted and optimized Layer 2 operations.

Capturing BPDU Traffic for Analysis

Bridge Protocol Data Units, or BPDUs, are the fundamental communication packets used by the Spanning Tree Protocol and its derivatives to maintain a loop-free Layer 2 topology. Analyzing BPDU traffic is one of the most effective ways to understand the behavior of STP, troubleshoot issues, verify root bridge elections, and validate that the network topology aligns with intended designs. Capturing BPDUs allows engineers to observe real-time protocol activity, track down misconfigurations, and diagnose network instabilities that may not be evident from switch logs or command-line interfaces. Because BPDUs operate at Layer 2 and are exchanged between directly connected switches, their analysis provides insight into the foundational processes that govern Ethernet switching behavior.

Capturing BPDU traffic begins with identifying the correct location in the network to observe these frames. Since BPDUs are sent to a multicast destination MAC address specifically reserved for spanning tree processes, they are not flooded across the network and typically do not reach hosts or endpoints. To capture BPDUs, one must mirror or span the traffic from a switch port that is actively participating in STP. Ideally, the capture should be performed on a trunk port or uplink between switches, where BPDUs are exchanged as part of the normal protocol operation. This provides visibility into the negotiation between switches, the advertisement of root bridge information, and the determination of port roles.

Using a protocol analyzer such as Wireshark, the capture device must be placed in a location that receives raw Layer 2 frames. The analyzer should be configured to listen promiscuously on the interface and apply display filters for BPDU frames. In Wireshark, a common filter to use is eth.dst == 01:80:c2:00:00:00 or stp, which displays all STP-related traffic. When the capture begins, the analyzer will display BPDU frames that include fields such as the root bridge ID, sender bridge ID, port ID, path cost, and timers. These fields are critical for determining the current topology and understanding why certain paths are chosen or blocked.

The root bridge ID is one of the most important elements within the BPDU. It contains both the bridge priority and the MAC address of the switch currently acting as the root bridge. If multiple switches are claiming to be the root bridge, or if the root bridge changes frequently, this is visible in the captured BPDUs. Frequent root bridge changes are a strong indicator of instability, misconfiguration, or a failure in the expected topology. By comparing the sender bridge ID to the root bridge ID, one can also determine how each switch views the network and whether it believes itself to be closer or further from the root.

Path cost is another essential field to examine during BPDU analysis. It reflects the cumulative cost from a given switch to the root bridge and helps determine which path should be used as the primary route. Lower path costs indicate preferred paths. Discrepancies in path cost may point to mismatched link speeds, incorrect cost assignments, or asymmetric routing behavior. Engineers can trace the progression of path costs across multiple switches in the topology by analyzing

BPDUs from different links, building a map of how traffic is expected to flow. This also aids in verifying whether STP has made the optimal forwarding decisions based on the current network layout.

Timer values included in the BPDU provide additional insight into protocol behavior. These include the hello time, max age, and forward delay timers. Unusual or inconsistent timer values across different switches can indicate either a misconfigured root bridge or inconsistencies in the protocol version running on each device. For example, a switch running Rapid Spanning Tree Protocol may exhibit different timer behavior compared to one running classic 802.1D STP. If timer values do not match what is expected for the protocol in use, the capture can highlight which switch is out of compliance and potentially causing instability.

BPDU captures also reveal the presence of topology changes. When a switch detects a topology change, it sets the topology change flag in its BPDU. This notifies other switches to shorten their MAC address aging times and prepare for changes in the forwarding database. If this flag is frequently set in the captured traffic, it may indicate that one or more ports are flapping, devices are moving between ports, or there is a recurring issue causing instability. Identifying which switch is generating the topology change notifications allows engineers to narrow the scope of investigation and focus on problematic segments of the network.

Another use case for BPDU capture is identifying unauthorized or rogue switches. If a device begins sending BPDUs with a low bridge priority in an attempt to become the root bridge, this will be visible in the capture. Engineers can examine the sender MAC address and trace the offending port through the network. This is particularly important in secure environments where network control must be tightly enforced. Capturing and analyzing BPDUs can serve as a method of intrusion detection, helping to prevent accidental or malicious disruptions to the spanning tree topology.

Captures can also help verify the impact of configuration changes. After modifying bridge priorities, adjusting port costs, or enabling features such as root guard or BPDU guard, engineers can analyze subsequent BPDUs to confirm that the intended behavior is taking place. For example, if a port is set to block BPDUs but is still forwarding them, a capture will immediately reveal the discrepancy. This real-time feedback ensures that the network operates as expected and that policy changes are successfully enforced.

In complex environments where MSTP or RSTP is deployed, BPDU analysis becomes even more informative. These protocols use additional fields and instance mappings that describe how VLANs are associated with spanning tree instances and how rapid transitions are handled. Capturing these enhanced BPDUs allows engineers to verify correct instance alignment, proper identification of root bridges per instance, and consistency in port roles. It also helps identify whether all switches agree on the MST region configuration, which includes the region name, revision number, and VLAN mappings. Any mismatch in these fields causes the affected switches to treat each other as belonging to different regions, resulting in blocked links and suboptimal forwarding.

Ultimately, BPDU analysis provides a detailed and reliable window into the operation of the spanning tree control plane. It enables proactive verification of network design, fast identification of anomalies, and informed troubleshooting during outages or instability. As networks grow more dynamic and complex, the ability to analyze low-level protocol behavior remains a crucial skill for engineers seeking to maintain robust and resilient Layer 2 topologies. By incorporating regular BPDU capture and review into network maintenance routines, organizations can gain better visibility, prevent future problems, and ensure that STP continues to function as a trusted foundation of Ethernet switching.

High Availability Design Patterns

Designing for high availability in networking environments is an essential practice for organizations that depend on uninterrupted access to digital services, applications, and communications. As systems become more interconnected and expectations for continuous uptime grow, the network infrastructure must be architected to tolerate faults, minimize downtime, and recover rapidly from failures.

High availability is not a single feature or protocol, but rather a design philosophy implemented through a collection of interconnected patterns that together ensure that no single point of failure can bring down critical services. These patterns apply at all layers of the network, from physical topology and link aggregation to Layer 2 redundancy, Layer 3 routing, and even application-layer resiliency.

One of the foundational principles of high availability is redundancy. Redundancy must be applied not just to devices but also to links, paths, and services. At the hardware level, this often includes deploying dual power supplies, redundant fans, and hot-swappable components in switches and routers. However, the network topology plays a far greater role. A common design pattern is the use of dual-homed connections, where each access switch or server connects to two upstream distribution or core switches. These uplinks form redundant paths so that the failure of a single device or interface does not isolate the connected systems. To support this model effectively, protocols such as LACP are used to bundle multiple links into a single logical connection, enabling load balancing while providing automatic failover in the event of link loss.

At Layer 2, high availability is typically achieved by designing topologies that incorporate loop-free redundancy. In legacy networks, this has traditionally been handled through the Spanning Tree Protocol, which blocks redundant links to prevent loops. However, modern high availability designs often bypass the limitations of STP by using technologies such as TRILL, SPB, or overlay networks like VXLAN. These protocols allow all links to remain active while still ensuring a loop-free environment. They also enable equal-cost multipathing, which distributes traffic across multiple available paths and enhances both performance and fault tolerance. In high-availability designs, access switches are connected to multiple aggregation points, and the fabric is constructed in a spine-leaf or Clos topology to support scalable and resilient traffic flows.

High availability at Layer 3 involves dynamic routing protocols that can quickly detect failures and reroute traffic. Interior Gateway Protocols such as OSPF and IS-IS provide fast convergence through link-state advertisements. They are capable of recalculating optimal paths within milliseconds when a change is detected. Exterior routing through BGP adds another layer of resilience, particularly in multi-homed environments where organizations connect to multiple ISPs. BGP policies and route filtering mechanisms ensure that traffic can continue to flow even if one provider becomes unavailable. In high-availability network designs, routing adjacency is maintained on redundant interfaces across different physical devices, ensuring that route updates can be propagated instantly when failures occur.

Another critical high availability pattern is the use of first-hop redundancy protocols such as HSRP, VRRP, and GLBP. These protocols provide fault tolerance for default gateway functionality at Layer 3. In a typical scenario, end devices are configured with a virtual IP address as their gateway, which is shared between two or more routers. One router actively forwards traffic, while the other remains in standby mode. If the active router fails, the standby router takes over the virtual IP, often within seconds, allowing end devices to continue communicating without requiring reconfiguration. These protocols are especially useful in campus and branch deployments where high availability is needed for client access but where dynamic routing might be overly complex.

Beyond protocol-level design, high availability is also enforced through operational patterns. Monitoring and alerting systems must be in place to detect anomalies and notify administrators of issues before they become outages. Health checks and keepalives between devices and services are used to validate that links and nodes are operational. When failures are detected, automated scripts or controllers may initiate failover procedures, update routing or forwarding tables, and even reconfigure firewall or security rules as needed. Integrating network infrastructure with automation and orchestration tools increases consistency, reduces response times, and minimizes human error during incident response.

Geographic redundancy is another advanced pattern used to ensure availability in the event of site-level disasters. This involves deploying duplicate infrastructure in separate physical locations, such as two data centers or cloud availability zones. These environments must be synchronized in terms of data and configuration so that one site can take over for the other with minimal service disruption. Technologies like stretch VLANs, redundant links over dark fiber, and data replication protocols support the extension of services across sites. Routing policies are often designed to prioritize local paths under normal conditions but shift traffic to remote sites when necessary. Load balancers, DNS-based traffic steering, and global server load balancing are frequently used to distribute connections between sites in real time.

Another key aspect of high availability is modular design. Networks built using modular principles isolate failures within defined boundaries, preventing cascading failures and simplifying recovery. For instance, if a failure occurs in one module or pod, it does not affect the operation of other modules. This segmentation also enhances security, as policies can be enforced at the boundary of each module. Modular designs often use identical building blocks that are easy to replicate and scale, which aligns well with automation and provisioning systems.

Application-aware networking further enhances high availability by enabling the network to prioritize and route traffic based on application performance or business relevance. In these architectures, quality of service is tightly integrated with failover strategies. For example, if a link or path degrades beyond acceptable latency or packet loss thresholds, high-priority traffic such as voice or transactional data can be rerouted through alternative paths with better performance. Modern network operating systems support telemetry and real-time analytics that inform these decisions dynamically, further improving the network's responsiveness to failures.

Service insertion and chaining, often used in software-defined environments, also support high availability by allowing services such as firewalls, load balancers, and WAN optimizers to be dynamically deployed or rerouted in response to network events. These services are no longer tied to fixed physical locations but can exist as virtual functions anywhere in the infrastructure. Their availability is managed through orchestration tools that monitor service health and redistribute traffic as needed to maintain continuity.

Ultimately, high availability design patterns are about anticipating failure and building networks that are resilient, adaptive, and maintain service continuity even under adverse conditions. These patterns reflect a comprehensive approach that spans device-level redundancy, protocol selection, operational practices, and business continuity planning. As digital dependency deepens across industries, mastering these patterns becomes fundamental to delivering secure, efficient, and always-on network services.

Loop Prevention in Large Ethernet Fabrics

In large-scale Ethernet fabrics, loop prevention is one of the most critical aspects of maintaining network stability and performance. Ethernet, by its nature, lacks a built-in mechanism for identifying and eliminating loops at Layer 2. When loops are present, even a single broadcast frame can endlessly circulate, consuming bandwidth and CPU resources until the network becomes overwhelmed in what is known as a broadcast storm. In small or moderately sized networks, traditional loop prevention mechanisms such as the Spanning Tree Protocol have served as the primary safeguard against these disruptions. However, as networks scale and demands for performance, convergence speed, and full-path utilization increase, newer methods and architectures have been developed to prevent loops in ways that are both more efficient and more compatible with high-density, high-throughput environments.

The classic approach to loop prevention in Ethernet is the deployment of STP or one of its more advanced variants like RSTP or MSTP. These protocols use bridge protocol data units to detect and logically block redundant links, thus ensuring a loop-free topology. In larger networks, however, this approach becomes increasingly inefficient. Spanning tree-based designs must sacrifice available bandwidth by placing some links into a blocking state. In topologies with dozens or hundreds of switches, this results in suboptimal path utilization and severely limits the potential for load balancing and high availability. Additionally, STP can take several seconds to reconverge after a topology change, an unacceptable delay in modern data centers where applications demand near-instantaneous failover and traffic rerouting.

To address the limitations of STP in large fabrics, loop prevention is achieved through alternative mechanisms that focus on proactive loop avoidance rather than reactive loop blocking. One such method is the use of link-state routing protocols at Layer 2, as implemented by TRILL and SPB. These protocols allow switches to exchange topology information and build a complete view of the network, enabling them to calculate shortest paths and ensure that traffic always follows a predictable, loop-free route. Because these protocols understand the entire network topology, they can prevent loops by intelligently selecting paths based on destination rather than relying on blocked ports and timers.

In TRILL networks, loop prevention is reinforced through the use of hop counts and the identification of ingress and egress RBridges. Every TRILL frame includes a hop count field that is decremented at each hop, ensuring that a frame cannot circulate indefinitely. If the hop count reaches zero, the frame is discarded. Additionally, TRILL frames carry the nickname of the ingress RBridge, allowing any receiving device to determine if the frame has already passed through the same point and should be stopped. This approach combines elements of routing logic with traditional Ethernet behavior, allowing TRILL to eliminate loops while preserving compatibility with standard Ethernet hosts and protocols.

SPB uses a similar strategy by leveraging IS-IS to build a link-state database and compute a loop-free forwarding tree for each service instance. SPB's capability to support multiple active topologies and virtualized services enables it to maintain loop-free operation even in densely meshed environments with numerous VLANs or service identifiers. Because SPB is inherently loop-avoiding rather than loop-breaking, it can use all available paths without the risk of broadcast storms or traffic duplication. This design makes it highly suitable for large fabric deployments, especially those that require multi-tenancy, service isolation, or geographically dispersed resources.

Overlay networks provide another layer of loop prevention in large Ethernet fabrics. Technologies such as VXLAN encapsulate Ethernet frames in IP packets, effectively moving forwarding decisions to the Layer 3 infrastructure. The use of point-to-point tunnels between VXLAN tunnel endpoints inherently avoids the possibility of loops, as each tunnel has a clearly defined source and destination. Control-plane protocols such as BGP EVPN distribute MAC address reachability information, further ensuring that traffic is delivered correctly without relying on flooding or learning through unknown unicast behavior. In these environments, loops are not prevented by blocking links or calculating spanning trees but by encapsulating and directing traffic within a controlled and loop-free overlay.

Operational practices also play a critical role in loop prevention. Network segmentation, whether by VLAN, VRF, or overlay constructs, limits the scope of any potential loop and reduces the blast radius of broadcast traffic. Where loops do occur due to configuration errors or unexpected changes, containment mechanisms such as storm control and broadcast suppression can limit their impact. These features monitor traffic levels on switch ports and apply rate limiting when excessive broadcast, multicast, or unknown unicast traffic is detected. While they do not prevent loops, they serve as important safety mechanisms to reduce collateral damage.

Access control at the network edge further strengthens loop prevention. In environments where end devices might connect using unmanaged switches or rogue equipment, features such as BPDU guard and root guard ensure that unauthorized devices cannot participate in the spanning tree topology or alter the network's logical structure. These protections are essential in campus and enterprise networks where user devices could potentially introduce loops, either inadvertently or maliciously. By enforcing strict policies at edge ports, the fabric can preserve its stability and prevent loops from forming at the periphery.

Advanced monitoring tools contribute significantly to proactive loop prevention. Real-time visibility into network topology, traffic flows, and protocol behavior enables administrators to detect anomalies before they cause outages. Tools that support SPAN or RSPAN, along with flow telemetry and packet capture, allow for detailed inspection of potential loop behavior. Some platforms incorporate loop detection algorithms that identify patterns consistent with looping traffic, such as repeated MAC address movement or identical frames arriving on multiple ports. Alerts and automated mitigation actions can be triggered when such patterns are detected, allowing for immediate response.

As Ethernet fabrics continue to grow in size and complexity, the role of automation and orchestration in loop prevention becomes more important. Automated provisioning ensures that VLANs, services, and routing protocols are consistently configured across the network. This consistency is vital in avoiding misconfigurations that could lead to bridging loops. Intent-based networking and controller-driven architectures further reduce the risk of human error by validating changes against defined policies before deploying them. These systems can simulate the impact of configuration changes in advance and prevent actions that would introduce loops or disrupt forwarding paths.

Preventing loops in large Ethernet fabrics requires a multifaceted approach that combines protocol design, topology planning, traffic engineering, and operational discipline. By moving beyond traditional spanning tree models and embracing modern technologies such as TRILL, SPB, and VXLAN, network designers can create environments that not only eliminate loops but also support full path utilization, fast convergence, and scalable service delivery. These architectures enable large-scale, high-performance Ethernet fabrics that meet the demands of virtualization, cloud computing, and distributed applications while maintaining the foundational requirement of loop-free operation.

Performance Tuning for Protocol Convergence

Protocol convergence is a critical performance aspect in any network infrastructure, especially in environments where uptime, failover speed, and traffic continuity are non-negotiable. Convergence refers to the time it takes for a network to detect a failure or a topology change, propagate the necessary information across devices, and reestablish optimal forwarding paths. While convergence is a function of both hardware and software behavior, its speed and reliability are predominantly determined by protocol configuration and operational tuning. As networks evolve into high-density, highly virtualized, and application-sensitive fabrics, tuning for convergence becomes a strategic necessity rather than a routine optimization. The difference between sub-second convergence and several seconds of downtime can translate into measurable business impact, affecting services ranging from voice and video to transactional data systems and cloud workloads.

Each layer of the network stack has its own convergence mechanics, and tuning requires a coordinated approach across protocols such as Spanning Tree Protocol, Rapid Spanning Tree Protocol, Multiple Spanning Tree Protocol, OSPF, IS-IS, and BGP. At Layer 2, STP and its faster alternatives are often the first line of defense against loops and link failures. Legacy STP suffers from slow convergence due to timer-based state transitions. Devices wait for multiple seconds to confirm topology changes, cycling through listening, learning, and forwarding states. To optimize performance, most networks adopt Rapid Spanning Tree Protocol, which introduces a handshake mechanism and a more aggressive approach to transitioning ports to the forwarding state. RSTP achieves faster convergence by assuming that point-to-point links can immediately forward traffic under predictable circumstances. Network engineers can enhance this behavior further by explicitly configuring edge ports using the portfast feature, which prevents unnecessary delay on access interfaces connected to hosts.

In RSTP and MSTP environments, tuning the hello time, forward delay, and max age timers can yield measurable improvements, but these must be done with caution. Reducing these values shortens detection and recovery time but also increases the risk of false positives and topology instability. The optimal settings often depend on link quality, switch performance, and overall topology size. For example, in small or medium-sized networks with high-speed links and reliable cabling, more aggressive timer settings may be used safely. In contrast, geographically dispersed topologies with variable latency may require more conservative values to avoid erratic convergence behavior.

At Layer 3, convergence involves dynamic routing protocols detecting interface state changes and recomputing routing tables. OSPF and IS-IS use link-state advertisements to flood topology changes and rely on the Dijkstra algorithm to recalculate shortest paths. Tuning for performance involves configuring fast hello intervals and dead timers to detect failures quickly. The default hello and dead timers in OSPF are typically 10 seconds and 40 seconds, respectively, but these can be reduced to values like 1 and 3 seconds for faster convergence. This change must be synchronized across all routers within a given area or domain, as mismatched timers lead to adjacency failures. Additionally, the SPF timers, which control the frequency of recalculation after topology changes, can be adjusted to allow more immediate response. The SPF delay, hold time, and incremental timers govern how quickly updates are processed and pushed into the forwarding plane. These settings should be calibrated to strike a balance between responsiveness and CPU overhead, as overly aggressive recalculation can burden processors and lead to flapping or instability in larger networks.

BGP convergence, while historically slower than IGPs, can also be significantly improved through configuration. BGP detects neighbor loss based on TCP session state, which is not inherently optimized for rapid failure detection. To enhance this behavior, BFD, or Bidirectional Forwarding Detection, is often deployed in tandem with BGP. BFD operates independently of the routing protocol and sends control messages at a high frequency to detect faults within milliseconds. When BFD is configured on BGP peers, the protocol is informed almost instantly of link or path failures, allowing for immediate session teardown and rerouting. BGP timers themselves, such as the keepalive and hold timers, can also be tuned for faster convergence, but they are limited by the TCP transport layer. In large-scale networks with hundreds or thousands of prefixes, route dampening and flap suppression mechanisms must also be adjusted to ensure that instability in one segment does not delay convergence across the entire system.

Another convergence factor is the behavior of the data plane and how quickly it reflects control plane changes. In modern switching platforms, features like fast reroute, Equal-Cost Multi-Path, and loop-free alternates enable traffic to be redirected instantly to alternate paths while the control plane converges. These features rely on precomputed backup paths or real-time loop avoidance logic to reduce the perceived convergence time from the perspective of applications. Enabling these capabilities and ensuring that network devices support hardware-based forwarding updates accelerates both failure recovery and traffic restoration. When properly configured, the result is a seamless failover experience even in large-scale fabrics.

The physical design of the network also influences convergence performance. Topologies that favor symmetry, consistent link speeds, and well-defined hierarchies are easier to converge than complex, asymmetrical, or poorly documented networks. Spanning tree domains should be minimized and isolated where possible, and routing areas or levels should be designed to contain instability within boundaries. Redistribution between protocols introduces latency and complexity, so careful filtering and summarization strategies should be implemented to limit the scope of topology changes. Designing with convergence in mind includes not just protocol selection but also consistent policy enforcement, modular layout, and the use of standardized configurations across devices.

Monitoring and testing are essential components of convergence tuning. Administrators must use telemetry, SNMP, NetFlow, or streaming analytics to observe convergence events, measure failover times, and identify bottlenecks. Tools such as event correlation engines and protocol analyzers help visualize the progression of changes and highlight where delay occurs. Lab simulations and failure drills are effective in validating convergence tuning before applying changes to production. These practices ensure that protocols react predictably under stress and that critical services remain available during transitions.

Ultimately, protocol convergence is both a science and an art. It demands an understanding of how each protocol operates, how it interacts with others, and how its behavior changes under load or during failures. Tuning convergence performance involves configuring timers, enabling supporting protocols, architecting the topology, and ensuring that the hardware is capable of supporting rapid updates. In high-stakes environments where latency and availability are tightly coupled to business outcomes, optimized convergence is not a luxury but a requirement. Engineers who master these tuning practices build networks that not only recover from failure with grace but also deliver a level of resilience that modern digital operations depend on.

Ethernet Redundancy Models Compared

Ethernet networks form the core of most enterprise and data center infrastructures, serving as the foundational medium for communication across devices, services, and applications. Given their central role, the ability of Ethernet networks to withstand failures and continue operating is paramount. This capability is largely achieved through redundancy—designing the network in such a way that no single point of failure can bring down connectivity. Over the years, various redundancy models have evolved to address the challenge of ensuring continuous service in the face of link, device, or topology failure. Comparing these models provides a clear view of their respective advantages, limitations, and use cases in modern network design.

The most basic redundancy model relies on the Spanning Tree Protocol, which was introduced to prevent loops in Ethernet networks by disabling redundant paths. Classic STP builds a single tree that spans the entire network, blocking all but one active path between switches. If the primary path fails, STP reconverges by unblocking one of the redundant paths. This method provides redundancy but sacrifices bandwidth efficiency because many links are left unused during normal operation. STP also suffers from relatively slow convergence times, which can take upwards of 30 seconds in default configurations. This delay is tolerable in small networks with low availability requirements but becomes a major concern in high-performance or latency-sensitive environments.

Rapid Spanning Tree Protocol was developed to improve upon the convergence times of STP. RSTP retains the loop prevention model of STP but significantly accelerates the process of moving ports into a forwarding state after a failure. It introduces edge ports, point-to-point link detection, and a rapid transition mechanism that allows ports to immediately become active when certain conditions are met. While this improves upon the original STP model, it still maintains the principle of blocking redundant links and does not allow for load balancing across those paths during normal operation. As a result, even RSTP-based redundancy models fall short in networks where full bandwidth utilization is critical.

Multiple Spanning Tree Protocol extends the capabilities of RSTP by allowing for multiple spanning trees to exist within the same physical topology. Each tree can be mapped to one or more VLANs, enabling different VLANs to use different active paths. This provides a limited form of load balancing and better resource utilization than single-instance STP or RSTP. However, the complexity of configuring and maintaining MSTP grows with the number of instances and VLAN mappings, making it less appealing in large-scale environments where automation and scalability are key priorities. MSTP is often used in campus networks or mid-sized enterprises that require predictable redundancy and can tolerate some degree of complexity for the benefit of improved efficiency.

EtherChannel, also known as Link Aggregation, presents a different model of redundancy by combining multiple physical links into a single logical interface. This model offers both redundancy and bandwidth aggregation, enabling traffic to be distributed across all active links simultaneously. If one of the links in the bundle fails, the remaining links continue to forward traffic without interruption. EtherChannel can be implemented statically or dynamically using the Link Aggregation Control Protocol. The advantage of this model is that it eliminates the need for STP to block any links and supports full utilization of available bandwidth. However, it is limited by the fact that all member links must terminate on the same pair of devices, which restricts its scalability and resilience in larger or more distributed topologies.

To overcome the limitations of traditional Layer 2 redundancy models, newer technologies such as TRILL and Shortest Path Bridging were introduced. These protocols replace the spanning tree paradigm with a link-state routing model, allowing all links in the network to be active and utilized simultaneously. TRILL uses IS-IS as its control plane and supports hop-by-hop forwarding based on the shortest path to the destination. Each TRILL switch, or RBridge, maintains a view of the entire topology and calculates optimal paths accordingly. This model offers fast convergence, loop-free forwarding, and full bandwidth utilization. SPB operates on similar principles and adds native support for multiple services, allowing for simpler provisioning and better traffic isolation. These redundancy models are well-suited for data center and carrier-grade networks where performance, scalability, and deterministic behavior are critical.

Overlay networks represent another modern approach to Ethernet redundancy. Technologies such as VXLAN create logical networks that are decoupled from the underlying physical topology. VXLAN tunnels encapsulate Ethernet frames within IP packets, allowing for dynamic routing of traffic across Layer 3 infrastructures. Redundancy is achieved by leveraging IP routing protocols and techniques such as Equal-Cost Multi-Path routing, enabling traffic to take any available path through the fabric. Failures are handled by the IP underlay, which reroutes traffic without impacting the overlay structure. This model is highly scalable and resilient but requires greater sophistication in design and operation. It is commonly used in cloud and virtualization environments where workload mobility and service availability are top priorities.

First Hop Redundancy Protocols add another layer of resilience by ensuring that end devices always have a reachable default gateway. Protocols like HSRP, VRRP, and GLBP allow multiple routers to present a single virtual IP address to clients. If the active gateway fails, another router automatically assumes the role, maintaining uninterrupted communication for connected devices. These protocols are not loop prevention mechanisms themselves but are essential components of an overall redundancy strategy, particularly at the network edge where devices depend on stable gateway access.

A final model to consider involves the use of redundant topologies at the physical level. This includes designs such as dual-homing and dual-core architectures, where each device or access switch connects to two separate upstream switches. This pattern is often found in spine-leaf topologies, where each leaf switch connects to multiple spine switches. Redundancy in this model is achieved through path diversity and intelligent routing rather than protocol behavior. The effectiveness of this design is enhanced when combined with routing protocols capable of fast failover and convergence, such as OSPF, IS-IS, or BGP. In environments where overlay networks are deployed, the physical topology serves as the high-availability backbone, while the overlay provides logical segmentation and service continuity.

Each Ethernet redundancy model has its strengths and trade-offs. Simpler models such as STP and RSTP are easy to deploy but inefficient in resource usage. More advanced models like TRILL, SPB, and VXLAN offer superior performance and resilience but require greater design expertise and operational oversight. The choice of model depends on factors such as network size, performance requirements, administrative resources, and the criticality of applications supported. In practice, many networks implement a combination of these models, layering different forms of redundancy across the topology to achieve a comprehensive and fault-tolerant design. The goal is not merely to survive failures but to maintain seamless service and predictable performance under all conditions. A well-architected redundancy strategy ensures that the network is not just operational, but robust, agile, and ready to support the demands of a connected enterprise.

www.ingramcontent.com/pod-product-compliance
Lightning Source LLC
LaVergne TN
LVHW051236050326
832903LV00028B/2437